(33)CR

£3-99

CW00662580

THE LAND OF EGYPT

Jasper More

THE LAND OF EGYPT

B. T. Batsford Ltd *London*

By the same author:

A Tale of Two Houses
The Land of Italy
The Mediterranean

First published 1980
© Jasper More 1980

ISBN 0 7134 1635 1

Printed and bound in Great Britain by
Redwood Burn Ltd
Trowbridge & Esher
for the publishers
B. T. Batsford Ltd, 4 Fitzhardinge Street, London W1H 0AH

CONTENTS

List of Illustrations   6
Acknowledgments   7
Map of Egypt   8
1 Practical   9
2 Historical — from Menes to Alexander   16
3 Alexandria   30
4 Historical — from Amr to Sadat   43
5 The Delta and Lower Egypt   61
6 Cairo   71
7 Ancient Egypt   90
8 From Cairo to Luxor   107
9 Luxor, Karnak and Thebes   122
10 From Luxor to Abu Simbel   139
11 Present and Future   150
Index   162

LIST OF ILLUSTRATIONS

Between pages 60-61
 1 Pompey's Pillar, Alexandria
 2 Cairo from the minaret of the Mosque of Ibn Tulun
 3 Mosque of Ibn Tulun
 4 Mosque of Sultan Hasan
 5 Cairo street scene
 6 Tomb-mosque of Kait Bey
 7 Village near Karnak
 8 The Sphinx
 9 The Meidum Pyramid
10 The Hypostyle Hall of the Temple of Seti
11 The Birth House of Horus
12 Obelisk of Queen Hatshepsut, Temple of Amun
13 Rameses II and his Wife, Temple of Amun
14 Tomb of Queen Hatshepsut, Deir el Bahari, Thebes
15 Statue of Horus the hawk god
16 Kom Ombo Temple
17 Donkey transport at Beni Hasan
18 The Colossi of Memnon
19 Feluccas at Assuan

Maps
  Egypt   page 8
  Cairo   facing page 71
  Luxor, Karnak and Thebes   facing page 138

ACKNOWLEDGMENTS

The Author and Publishers would like to thank the following for supplying the photographs reproduced in this book:
Douglas Dickins nos. 7, 11, 12, 13, 14, 15, 16, 17, 19
A. F. Kersting nos. 1, 2, 3, 4, 5, 6, 8, 9, 10, 18

Map of Egypt

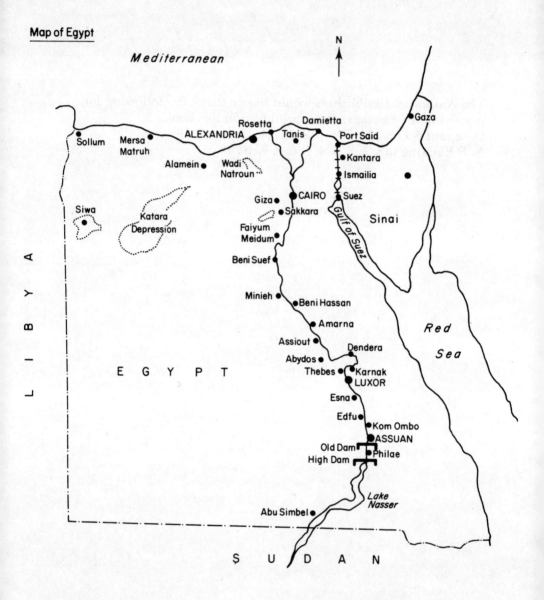

1 PRACTICAL

Egypt is a country that has been over thirty years at war; it is a Moslem country; and it is an Arab country; three factors all of which have implications for the traveller from abroad.

The state of war lasted a whole generation. There were four brief and violent outbreaks of active hostilities and though a settlement has been achieved there must always be the risk of further outbreaks with all that that implies. By contrast there have been during this period thousands of visitors—tens or even hundreds of thousands—who have happily seen the country without any awareness that the apparent state of peace could be suddenly and violently dispelled.

One Egyptian province, Sinai, has still at the time of writing not been released from enemy hands. The traffic in the recently re-opened Suez Canal could again be at risk. The realities of wartime, even if they were not apparent to the visitor, had to be lived with by the Egyptian authorities and in this context the authorities must be in large part military. Happily nothing of this situation need concern the tourist who keeps to the broad and beaten tourist track. But more enterprising spirits must remember that there are such things as forbidden zones, military enclaves and armed sentries: before leaving the broad and beaten tourist track it will always be prudent to enquire. What must be the concern of every tourist are the formalities of entry and inevitably these are more complicated in a country that has been so long at war. For this reason, and for others to be later stated in this chapter, an Egyptian visit needs to be planned well in advance.

Egypt is also a Moslem country. For a long period after the traumas of the Crusades and the Turkish wars Mahommedanism and Christianity had settled down side by side in existences that were fairly self-contained. Now Islam and the Western world have been violently thrown together with the third dimension of Russia and the Iron Curtain countries. It was long the fashion to laugh off Islam as a religion of flying carpets, tarbushes, minarets and Arabian Nights but the reality is different. Islam is a religion on the march and as a proselytising force it is probable that it is now making more progress than Christianity. Already it claims a thousand million followers. What has thrown the religions to-gether more than anything has been the Age of Oil. For the first time in centuries the Moslems are becoming the paymasters. And the strains on the Moslem world are evident. In a world in which oil magnates luxuriate in unexampled magnificence, wives who commit adultery are still liable to stoning, those who drink alcohol are publicly caned and thieves are punished by the cutting off of a hand. In fairness to Egypt the strains here are less evident. Egypt is not one of the oil-rich countries and the Moslem laws are tempered. The visitor nevertheless needs to be constantly aware that he is in the presence of a religion which, so far from being laughed off, must be confronted as one of the most formidable, vital and expanding religions of the twentieth century world.

Notwithstanding its claim of unity, the Moslem religion does not impose equal sanctions in all its countries. In Egypt women are not compelled to wear the veil, unbelievers are not excluded from the mosques, native quarters are not barred to foreigners. Yet certain precautions need to be observed. When entering mosques it is usual that shoes must be left behind; when visiting native quarters it is as well to have a guide; when seeking in-formation it is better to approach a man rather than a woman. Friday is a day of Moslem religion and Ramadam is a month of Moslem fasting and both need to be respected. When five times a day the extraordinary wailing call to prayer is issued from the minaret (in theory by the muezzin, more frequently in fact by gramophone record or cassette) it is better not to laugh. Nor when seeking information about a mosque can one buttonhole the equivalent of a vicar or a parish priest; nothing comes between a Mahommedan and his God and one's best recourse is to the Imam, the functionary responsible for funerals and weddings.

Egypt also is an Arab country. This taken literally is a more questionable statement. In the seventh century AD the country was indeed conquered by the Arabs but there is no evidence to suggest that the native population was exterminated so that Arabs could take their place. Obviously there was some infusion of Arab blood, but substantially the original population must have re-mained. What concerns us is that through the centuries the Egyptians acquired the Arab religion, the Arab outlook and the Arab tongue. With the flowing tide of Arab conquest sweeping right across North Africa to the Atlantic Ocean Egypt became also geographically the centre of the Arab world. The facts of geography were recognised during periods in the Middle Ages when Cairo became the seat of the Caliphs of the whole of Islam. Then the Turkish conquest supervened and it was not until the expulsion of the Turks in the present century that Egypt resumed her true place in the Arab world.

It is only in very recent years that Egypt has re-acquired a truly Arab character. For almost a hundred years, from the mid-nineteenth century to the mid-twentieth, Egypt was in some degree bossed by foreigners, French financiers, English administrators, German and Swiss hotel-keepers, Greek and Italian traders. Much of this has been changed by the great confiscations and nationalisations of the 1950s and 1960s. And for the visitor this has serious implications. There is no people more lovable than the Arabs or more genuine but people however lovable and genuine have their defects and the visitor must face them. The greatest defect of the Arab is lack of staying-power. The detailed application of the German, the conscientious attention to detail of the Swiss, the long views of the self-interested British are totally foreign to his nature. Creature of impulse, and reaction, and passion, he is totally unsuited to the running of those enterprises which call for poise, breadth of vision and the long view. Coming down to brass tacks, Arabs are temperamentally unsuited in the arts of the tourist trade, not excluding the running of hotels.

Not that the Arabs are incapable of great initiatives and imaginative enterprise: far from it. The difficulty comes when the original initiative or enterprise has succeeded and needs to be kept in being. It may be a characteristic of great peoples to lose interest in a project once achieved but for the customer it has its disadvantages. With the termination of European control many landmarks of the tourist's Egypt have dwindled or vanished. With the new Arab initiatives and enterprises a new rule must be followed; no longer the harking back to that charming traditional milieu of which parents and grandparents spoke so nostalgically; now the only safety is in the up-to-date. The new rule must always be to patronise the establishment of today that has already updated the establishment of yesterday.

For the prospective traveller who thinks that he can, so to speak, visit Egypt on the loose the consequences are formidable. Not available to him are those welcoming small hotels of Western Europe so conveniently spaced along every few miles of his journey. Not for him are those restaurants where one can drop in with confidence for a meal of well recognisable dishes. Difficult to find would be the equivalent of the British pub. Except in the great cities—Cairo and Alexandria—and the great tourist resorts —Luxor and Assuan—the hotel that is first class or even tolerable by Western standards hardly exists. For the tourist who seeks to leave the beaten track there is not only required a knowledge of Arabic or an interpreter, but also a capacity to endure the conditions implied by Youth Hostels, tents or native hotels. And all this implies one constraint on Egyptian travel; it almost excludes the motor tour.

Not that there is any difficulty in driving from Cairo to Alexandria; there is a good road through the Delta and a good road through the desert. Nor is there any difficulty in driving to Suez (if one wants to drive to Suez). Nor is there any difficulty about the Pyramids or Sakkara. The challenge begins when one confronts the trip to Upper Egypt. The journey to Luxor is too long a trip for an Egyptian day; eked out with calls at intermediate sites of interest, it becomes impossible. The tourist to Upper Egypt is thrown back on the tent or the caravan: alternatively on the aeroplane, the train or the ship. A day plane or a night train will take him in reasonable comfort from Cairo to Luxor or Assuan; but once again he loses the prospect of the intermediate sites. The traveller who wants to see the most of the Nile Valley without roughing it is thrown back upon the ship. The Nile ships are not luxury liners; property of the Egyptian government, they are leased out to entrepreneurs who are concerned to see that standards of punctuality, cleanliness and cuisine are maintained. Limited in number, they are enormously sought after by the tourists of the world; hence a second reason for planning the Egyptian tour well in advance.

The third reason for making plans early is of course Health and this brings up the whole question of Egyptian climate. 'Yes, it usually is sunny here' Lord Kitchener is said to have replied to a Nile steamer passenger who imprudently asked whether it was not a nice sunny day. The sun obviously is the principle climatic antagonist in Egypt but it is important not to be misled into the idea that every day in Egypt is like a fine afternoon in an English June.

Alexandria and the Mediterranean littoral can present a very different aspect. This part of Egypt in winter is no different from any other part of the Mediterranean; that is to say, there can be plenty of nice sunny days but it can also be cold and wet and there can be fearsome gales. Much of the Delta has the same climatic conditions. By the time one gets to Cairo things have altered; it can still be cold in December and January but the wet days will be few. As one progresses into Upper Egypt wet days will be exceptional but it can still be chilly. This is due to the curious climatic cause that Egypt lives almost permanently with the north wind. Some beneficient deity of Ancient Egypt must have ordained that this was so for the benefit of travellers to Upper Egypt; it meant before the days of steam that if you wanted to sail upstream you hoisted sail and if you wanted to sail downstream you lowered it. All this is of importance today for the Winter Season is still the most fashionable and it means that its addicts need always to be within reach of their pullover or shawl.

At the other extreme July and August will be barely tolerable on the Mediterranean coast. In Cairo they will be tolerable only if one is within instant reach of a swimming pool or shower. In the desert and in Upper Egypt the high summer is not tolerable at all for those who are not acclimatised. What then is left for the traveller? Spring and Autumn. February should be one of the golden months of Upper Egypt; May and June may be already too hot. Why not then March or April? March and April can be ideal but they are the treacherous months. Suddenly the north wind may fail, the sirocco may take over and for days on end the traveller may find himself buffeted and tortured by the Khamsin, the hot wind of the south suffocating in its temperature and even more suffocating from the clouds of desert sand with which it covers its victims. Why not then September, October and November? September can be delightful in Cairo, it is still too hot at Assuan; perhaps it is October and November that are the perfect months for Egypt as a whole.

We return to the problem of Health. Millions of Egyptian natives live happily in the Delta and Valley without, as far as one knows, being ever in need of summoning the family doctor. In the Second World War there were many turns and twists of fortune but none of them, so far as is recorded, were due to armies being prostrated with local disease. For the modern traveller transported suddenly into a completely unfamiliar climate the challenge is severe. A multiplicity of horrific ailments hover round him, smallpox, typhoid, dysentery, bilharzia. Months in advance it is necessary to go into consultations with one's doctor, to discuss the pros and cons of rival remedies, to arm oneself with pills and learn by heart the rules of prudence and of health. The result of all this probably is that on one's tour one will be smitten with nothing worse than gyppy tummy but the tourist will be lucky who completes the tour with a completely clean bill of health.

The necessary precautions begin with vaccination and a multitude of inoculations and for these obviously a time factor is relevant. They continue after one's arrival with necessary precautions about food and drink and these involve some of the saddest deprivations; fresh fruit and raw vegetables must all be suspect and only in the most guaranteed circumstances can one drink anything not contained in a bottle or a can. The western stomach is also a soft target for cooking of an unfamiliar style. The result is that mealtimes must be a matter of international cooking of the type of western hotels or else of hazardous excursions into the native vernacular. In the matter of drinks, by contrast, there is a simple rule, conditioned by the appalling rates of Egyptian import duties; never drink anything that is not native. There is fortunately a wide choice of Egyptian products and many of them are excellent; delicious fruit juices abound, there is a very satisfactory Egyptian beer and by careful experiment it is possible to find highly palatable Egyptian wines. All this in a Moslem country where in theory alcohol is taboo. The saddest deprivation in the Upper Egypt tour is that it is absolutely unsafe to bathe in the Nile.

Finally, in contemplation of an Egyptian visit, it is necessary to consider what things to take to the country and what things to bring away. The restrictions of air travel and the climate of the country both suggest clothes that are not too heavy. For the traveller to Upper Egypt by far the most important consideration is footwear and rope soles and rubber soles should by no means be excluded nor anything that is loose and light. The modern vogue for hatlessness also needs to be reconsidered with the challenge of the Egyptian sun. Dark glasses are necessary adventitious aids and no Egyptian tourist will omit his camera and his torch.

As to what to bring back it is more difficult to advise. The visitor to the Bazaar in Cairo will have pressed upon him an amazing quantity and variety of objects some of which can be seen being hand-made. Not all Westerners are appreciative of modern Arab metalwork but more attention may well be given to some of the articles in leather. In Upper Egypt some individual villages have their own trades and one may find oneself buying unexpectedly attractive wicker work and a variety of earthenware. More surprisingly at Luxor or Assuan is the opportunity to buy ladies' dresses known as *gallabiya*. A more serious challenge is posed by the 'antiquities' with which the traveller is assailed at every turn. With laudable enterprise the Cairo museum has a sales department of things it guarantees as genuine and for the tourist who is determined to come back with some relic of Ancient Egypt this is certainly the safest buy.

Egypt is a section of the Orient transported to North Africa and in dealings with Egyptians the conventions of the Orient must apply. The first requisite of the visitor is patience, the second good humour, the third a lively sense of the fact that he must always be guarding his wicket. Purchases in Egypt are not made at a price, they are made after elaborate and time-consuming bargaining. Bakshish is a word still much in use and appeals for it must be dealt with by a subtle mixture of sympathy and firmness. For those who wish to explore Oriental living there is no one to gainsay them; exploration must be gradual and must progress step by step, from the bazaar to the café, from the café to the hammam, from the hammam to the night club, from the night club, if one is fortunate, to a private Oriental house. Amidst much that is squalid and depressing the feature which will emerge is that Egyptians manage to remain cheeful and friendly. And it will not be long before the stranger finds amidst all discouragements that this is a country he has come to love.

2 HISTORICAL – FROM MENES TO ALEXANDER

Egypt has a longer recorded history than any other country of the western world but inevitably its beginnings are shrouded in mystery and doubt. Much learned ink has been expended upon the question whether the ancestors of the Egyptians were in origin African or Asiatic. The question now may seem to be not of great importance; what is generally accepted is that a human population occupied, while they were still habitable by humans, the desert plateaux on the two sides of the Nile; and that it was only when, by changes of rainfall and climate, these areas ceased to be habitable, that the inhabitants began to colonise the river valley itself.

Both valley and Delta were originally uninhabitable marsh and bog. With the infinite adaptability of the human race the plateaux dwellers became cultivators, gradually reclaimed the land of the valley and the Delta to make it arable land; and in the course of centuries established themselves as settled communities along the whole course of the Nile.

A more singular form of agricultural economy it would be difficult to conceive. Since the valley was virtually without rainfall, it would have become a desert but for the constant supply of water from the Nile. Yet no water supply could have been more inconstant; the annual phenomenon of the Nile was the great inundation which began to reach Assuan on the Egyptian frontier about the beginning of June and Cairo some weeks later and generally rose to its maximum height in September and October. The Egyptian peasant would sow his crops as the inundation subsided towards the end of the year and would complete his harvest by the end of May; his land would then be overwhelmed by the flood and he himself would have to retire to the safety of his village above flood level. As the inundation subsided, major works of reclamation and reconstruction might be needed to bring the land back into use before the next sowing. The enormous benefit of this extraordinary annual sequence was the annual deposit of silt brought down by the flood which both fortified and manured the valley soil. What was always painfully evident was that the flood

level could not be relied on; if it was too high, great damage could
be done; if it was too low, the land ceased to be fertile. The reason
for the phenomenon has always been the tremendous rainfall which
in springtime descends on the mountains of Ethiopia where the
Blue Nile has its source.

The earliest political organisations appear to have been the two
kingdoms of Upper and Lower Egypt, each of which was divided
into nomes, a name which has survived to the present day. All this
had happened more than three thousand years before Christ when
Egyptian history officially began.

So enormous a span of human history needs firm organisation
and fortunately this has been provided. Manetho, a Greek living
shortly after the time of Alexander the Great, provided a framework for Egyptian history which still endures today. He divided
the whole period of some three thousand years between thirty
Dynasties up to the time of Alexander himself. And out of these
thirty Dynasties were selected three groups of special importance
which are known to us respectively as the Old, the Middle and the
New Kingdoms.

The founder of Egyptian history, according to Manetho, was
King Menes who lived about 3200 BC. He it was who first united
Lower and Upper Egypt and made the country into a single
kingdom. Tradition credits him with having been the first founder
of the capital city of Memphis, where he is said to have built a
fortress and also a temple in honour of the God Ptah. One would
like to identify his tomb; one suggestion has been a large brick
mastaba near Qûs excavated by M. de Morgan in 1897. Menes was
the first Pharaoh of the First Dynasty.

His successors of the First and Second Dynasties are known to
have established their tombs at Abydos, the most sacred place of
Ancient Egypt. But a bold departure was made by Zoser the first
Pharaoh of the Third Dynasty who definitely established his capital
at Memphis and built his tomb not far away at Sakkara. This was
the famous Step-Pyramid, still one of Egypt's major tourist attractions. The tradition of the Step-Pyramid is that it was designed
and built under the inspiration Zoser's adviser and architect
Imhotep. It has the distinction of being the world's first building
built of stone; though always a 'Step-Pyramid,' its surfaces originally
were sheathed with fine casing stones, so as to make its exterior a
series of glacis.

The example of Zoser was soon followed. Under the Fourth
Dynasty the power of Egypt grew and its first Pharaoh Snefru

built two pyramids, one at Meidum and one at Dashur. Meidum is credited with being, architecturally speaking, the first true pyramid and rose to a height of over 200 feet; Dashur, over 300 feet in height, approaches the size of the Great Pyramid of Giza. The Great Pyramid was the work of Cheops, the successor of Snefru; the other two pyramids of Giza were the works of later Pharaohs of the same dynasty, Chephren and Mykerinos. This dynasty finished about 2500 BC.

The Pyramids, particularly those of Cheops and Chephren, are so enormously larger than any other construction of unaided human hands that the question has obviously been debated as to how they were built; more particularly, since Egypt was not by modern standards a large or wealthy country, what was the economic, social and religious structure that made possible such gigantic undertakings—undertakings that were, after all, only the tombs of single individuals? Herodotus states that in the construction of the Great Pyramid 100,000 men were occupied for twenty years, and that they worked for three months in every year. Clearly the undertaking was made possible only by the uniquely eccentric habits of the Nile. During the three months of the annual inundation no agricultural work was possible and the peasants could be employed elsewhere. But was the method, as Cheops' enemies have asserted, the use of forced labour? Or was it, as his supporters like to suggest, a colossal charitable venture in aid of unemployment relief? Or was the Egyptian economy built up on slavery? Whatever may be the truth, it is impossible to believe that so gigantic an enterprise could have been even contemplated without an enormous measure of dedication on the part of all concerned. How was this brought about? The Pyramid we know was part of religion, intimately involved with other structures in the all-important process of securing the Pharaoh in the after-life. But the Pharaoh was, as far as we know, only a secular ruler. One would like to know much more about the religious and priestly organisation of the Old Kingdom. Mercifully the materials do not exist for a socio-economic study of the Old Kingdom such as would be fashionable in our present age.

The story of the Old Kingdom finishes with the Fifth and Sixth Dynasties. Their Pharaohs continued to build pyramids, generally at Sakkara or Abusir, but no longer on the scale of Cheops and Chephren. It is not possible, clearly, to know the details of a civilisation separated from us by so great an expanse of time. Nevertheless, thanks to certain peculiar aptitudes of the ancient

Egyptians, much has survived from these dynasties and it is possible to visualise some general impressions. The art of sculpture was already developed; the statue of Chephren in the Cairo museum is a strikingly lifelike reproduction of a king; and the Eygptians had already developed their custom, which runs through all the Egyptian periods, of recording by carved reliefs on the walls of tombs and temples the settings and activities of their daily lives. None of these is more striking than the tomb of Ti, an important official of the early part of the Fifth Dynasty, which we shall see at Sakkara. Here in literal details are the processes of Egyptian agriculture, estate management, fishing and fowling; as well the processes of the religious ceremonies of the time. Not the least fascinating aspect of this oft-seen type of Egyptian art is the combination of the childlike fidelity of the scenes with the astonishing expertise of the execution.

The Sixth Dynasty ended about 2,600 BC with Pharaoh Pepi II who we are asked to believe reigned for ninety-four years. From this time the historians date what they term the First Intermediate Period, to which are assigned the Seventh to Tenth Dynasties inclusive. All this is another way of saying that we have now reached a period — extending some three hundred years — of which very little is known. But some of these Pharaohs seem to have made a capital at Heracleopolis, a site near the modern Beni Suef, rejoicing now in an Arab name meaning 'Mother of Dust Heaps', which sufficiently describes it.

Egyptian history comes again to life with the Middle Kingdom which is defined as comprising the Eleventh and Twelfth Dynasties. The Eleventh Dynasty appears to have established itself at Thebes which now made its first mark in Egyptian history. From Thebes they appear to have extended their power northwards, eliminating Heracleopolis and establishing their rule over the whole of Upper and Lower Egypt. It was with the Eleventh Dynasty that began that series of tombs and temples which has made the western side of the Nile at Thebes the most remarkable architectural assemblage of the world. Much overshadowed by the more magnificent constructions of later ages, the mortuary temples of Mentuhotep II and Mentuhotep III have preserved sufficient of their outline to enable us to reconstruct a vision of tombs and chapels, colonnade and pyramid which must have made an impressive complex.

The Twelfth Dynasty was grander still and spread its architecture over many Egyptian cities, as well as projecting its rule over distant territories in Nubia and in Asia. Its Pharaohs also revived the pyramid cult. At Lisht, south of Dashur, were those of Amenemmes I and Sesostris I; Sesostris II built himself a pyramid at Lahun near the Faiyum; Sesostris III followed suit at Dashur itself; and Amenemmes III was responsible for the dynasty's greatest master-piece in his pyramid at Hawara in the Faiyum. The latter pyramid was combined with the famous Labyrinth, a subterranean burial chamber with a funerary temple covering some hundred acres and universally regarded by the Ancients—and even by those who had seen the pyramids at Giza—as being the greatest of all the wonders of Ancient Egypt.

The Twelfth Dynasty can be appreciated on a more human scale at Beni Hassan, about one hundred miles south of Cairo, where a series of rock-tombs of local dignitaries remain in good preservation. The Middle Kingdom also makes distinguished contributions to the Egyptian museums. Royal portraiture becomes a speciality and it is conjectured that the peculiar art of the sculptors was a product of the technical ability of Memphis inspired by the realism of Thebes.

With the Thirteenth or Fourteenth Dynasty Egyptian history takes a dive into the second of its so-called Intermediate Periods. This is the age of the Hyskos, rulers of whom little is known but much hatred is spread. They appear in fact to have been a family of Bedouins or Shepherds of Semitic origin, who established their power in the North while a rival dynasty maintained its rule at Thebes. Much learned disputation has concerned itself with the Hyskos, upon the question whether their eventual expulsion was connected with the Biblical story of Exodus. At any rate they were expelled and Egyptian history gets back onto an even keel.

We now reach the New Kingdom and the date of approximately 1550 BC. The New Kingdom is generally taken as covering six Dynasties, from the Eighteenth to the Twenty-Third, and it certainly covered the years which, so far as can be judged from the surviving remains, were the most splendid in the history of Ancient Egypt. The first three Pharaohs of the Eighteenth Dynasty, Ahmose, Amenophis I and Tuthmosis I, devoted themselves to the re-unification and expansion of the country; successful ex-peditions were mounted into Nubia; and Palestine was not only conquered but made into a kind of buffer state against the Asiatic powers beyond. The death of Tuthmosis II was followed by a confused succession in which the dominating character was his own widow Hatshepsut. This formidable lady, reigning first as regent for her young brother, soon displaced him and established herself as Queen, the first in the history of the Pharaohs. Her reign was by no means unsuccessful but in preference to military expeditions to Palestine she concentrated on commercial ventures to Punt (the modern Abyssinia) and to ambitious building projects near her own capital.

The Pharaohs of the New Kingdom had abandoned the idea of the pyramid. A completely new practice of royal sepultures was now instituted within close reach of the capital city of Thebes. By contrast with the ultra-conspicuous pyramid the new royal tombs were to be secreted away from human view so that they might never be discovered or violated. The chosen site for this purpose was the famous Valley of the Kings. The precautions of the Pharaohs were not proof against either the tomb-robbers of antiquity or the Egyptologists of modern times and thanks to modern excavations the plan of these New Kingdom tombs is well known. A dressed stone doorway totally hidden under mounds of earth and rubble would give access to a long passageway sloping steeply downwards and thence after a number of twists and turns to a series of excavated chambers, sometimes on the scale of a complete house, amongst which was the burial chamber. But this was only half the scheme, for a funerary temple had also to be provided. This was normally done some distance from the Valley of the Kings on the edge of the cultivated area of the Nile plain. For this reason few of them have survived.

Queen Hatshepsut's temple is a remarkable exception. For it she, or her architect Senmut, selected a site not on the Nile valley plain but against the background of the enclosing desert cliffs. The temple has in large part 'survived and is one of the most sensational of all the sights of Ancient Egypt. Neither this nor her other activities appear to have been approved by her brother and successor Tuthmosis III. He it was who initiated the practice which becomes so familiar under the New Kingdom of hacking out any honorific reliefs or inscriptions of his predecessor and sometimes substituting for them his own. In his defence it may be said that his sister's negligence put on him the task of recovering much of Egypt's former standing in Western Asia. As a builder he certainly rivalled Queen Hatshepsut, as we shall see when we come to visit Thebes. He is thought by some to have been the greatest of the Pharaohs.

Tuthmosis III was followed by Amenophis II, Tuthmosis IV and Amenophis III, under all of whom the tradition of great building was maintained. It was Amenophis III who by building

his mortuary temple on the edge of the Nile plain has been responsible for bequeathing to posterity the two colossal statues known
as the Colossi of Memnon. But these Pharaohs and probably their
predecessors may also have been responsible for a development
which was to lead to a remarkable reaction in Egyptian history.
This was the cult of Amun.

Amun, as we shall see, was not one of the original great gods of
Egyptian tradition. He first appears specifically as the god of
Thebes and it was doubtless the establishment of the New
Kingdom's capital at Thebes that led to his exaltation. It would be
interesting to know how far these Pharaohs were the masters, and
how far the servants, of the new cult. What is clear is that it led to
a development of building on a scale which had probably not
been seen in Egypt since the Pyramids and the Labyrinth. The
conclusion seems inescapable that this cult must have been accompanied by a great accession of priestly power.

A violent reaction occurred under the next Pharaoh Amenophis
IV. This period is certainly the most fascinating of Ancient Egypt
and it is tantalising that we do not know more about it. What is
clear is that the new Pharaoh removed himself completely from
Thebes and founded a great new capital at Amarna some two
hundred miles to the north. What is also clear is that he proclaimed
himself the champion of a new religion and, spurning the worship
of Amun, dedicated himself to the worship of a new deity, the sun-
god Aten, in honour of whom he changed his own name to
Akhenaten. Following the example of his predecessor he devoted
much labour to excising honorific inscriptions in honour of the
god he had dethroned; more importantly he erected in honour
of the new god a magnificent temple in the new capital. As we
shall see when we come to Amarna, there is little that survives—or
perphaps was permitted to survive—of his building activities. The
achievement nevertheless, was clearly considerable; in a reign of
not more than twenty years he established a city some five miles
long by one mile broad. The repercussions to which all this led
cannot be described because we do not know the details but they
can be imagined and perhaps never better than when listening to
the music of *Aida.*

Why does one waste time and writing on this brief interlude
which may only have been the expression of the ego of an eccentric
or fanatic? The answer is because of the astonishing quality of the
objects which have survived from his regime. The portrait of
Akhenaten himself discovered (strangely) at Karnak, with his

prominent cheek-bones and elongated chin; the bust of his wife Queen Nefertiti with her exquisite features and singularly expressive eyes; these are but the most famous and prominent of a whole school of art which provides the most vivid contrast with the vernacular tradition of Ancient Egypt. One of his portraits, now in the Luxor museum, comes nearer than anything else in Egypt to the poet's phrase 'the sneer of cold command.'

His successor was the boy king Tutankaten. Once again it is easier to imagine than to describe the passions and commotions that must have been unloosed in a new reign with so young a ruler. But clearly the battle was won by the priests of Amun. Amarna was abandoned, the capital was brought back to Thebes, the young Pharaoh himself had to change his name to Tutankhamen before dying at about the age of eighteen. It is one of the ironies of Egyptian history that by the modern discovery of his tomb virtually intact in the Valley of the Kings this obscure youth has become the most famous of the Pharaohs.

One would like to know more of Horemheb who after a short interval succeeded him. We know that he was a general and it must be assumed that he was not of royal blood. An immense activity seems to have been the character of his reign and the conclusion is that the era of Akhenaten must have produced an immense confusion. Clearly Horemheb both supported, and was supported by, the priests of Amun once again dominant in Egypt. From the little we know of him it seems clear that he not only restored order and re-conquered lost provinces but also paved the way for the great Pharaohs of the Nineteenth Dynasty and the ultimate triumphs of the priests of Amun.

It was the first Pharaoh of the Nineteenth Dynasty who brought into Egyptian history one of its most famous names, Rameses; but his reign was only brief and he was succeeded by his son Seti I. Seti was clearly a great ruler and waged war with success on the side of Asia. Four campaigns are recorded, principally against the rising power of the Hittites, and since the end of his reign was peaceful we may assume that they were successful. Seti was also a great builder and his name should be cherished by the modern sightseer; fortunate in the artistic and architectural talent of his time, his name is associated with some of Egypt's most congenial buildings, notably his great temple at Abydos. He died sufficiently young to make possible a long reign for his son the celebrated Rameses II.

It could be tempting for connoisseurs of French history to see in Horemheb, Seti I and Rameses II the parallel with the great century of France under Henri IV, Louis XIII and Louis XIV.

Horemheb, like Henri IV, re-established order and authority and also managed to bring an to an end the religious dissensions which had ruined the country. Seti I, like Louis XIII, not only conducted successful wars abroad but also gave his name to one of the great periods of art and architecture. Rameses II did not quite equal Louis XIV's reign of seventy-two years but he succeeded at a more advanced age and his effective reign—of sixty-three years —was even longer. Like Louis XIV he performed in foreign wars and like Louis XIV he expected his achievements, in reality some-what modest, to be constantly glorified by the artists of his reign.

Their two reigns had other similarities, not all of them happy. First, Rameses II, like Louis XIV, was the greatest of all the royal builders. We do not know if there was an Egyptian Versailles for the palaces of the Pharaohs have not survived. But in terms of temples, this was the greatest age of Ancient Egyptian building. Memphis, Thebes, Abydos, Bubastis all witnessed his activity; above all his reign is associated with the gigantic undertakings of Luxor, Karnak and Abu Simbel. Adding up all the surviving architecture of Ancient Egypt, it has been estimated that one half of it dates from the reign of Rameses. Secondly, and this is a less congenial parallel, this is the reign of bombast. Everything had to be personalised to the greater glory of Rameses. His appearance at the battle of Kadesh against the Hittites, in which disaster was in fact only narrowly averted, had to be glorified by the artists of his reign in terms of a major victory. An even less congenial habit, by no means confined to Rameses II, became also a dominant feature of the reign—the practice of claiming as his own, by the simple expedient of erasing names and titles of predecessors and substituting his own, many of the great buildings of the preceding reigns (a technical term for which is 'usurping').

Thirdly, and sadly, it becomes apparent that the artistic level of his father's reign was not maintained. By comparison with the refined and imposing works of the reign of Seti much of what we see in the reign of Rameses and particularly in the later years is coarse and clumsy. Fourthly, and this is by inference, the reign must have been largely conditioned by the religious dogmatism of the Pharaoh. There was no Edict of Nantes to be revoked but the reign must evidently have been a conscious partnership between the Pharaoh and the priests and the gigantic constructions which were its fruit must have been as burdensome to the country as gratifying to all those involved in ministering to Amun. Fifthly, and this seems the inevitable conclusion, the resources of the country were overstrained and the death of Rameses was followed by a period of decline; and though spasmodic revival occurred under later rulers, the full power and splendour to which Rameses succeeded was never fully restored.

His son and successor Mineptah faced once more a serious situation in Asia and elsewhere and long campaigns had to be undertaken against Hittites, Libyans and Ethiopians, but in the end the Pharaoh prevailed. But thereafter the Dynasty dwindled, we know little or nothing of the successors of Mineptah and within one generation of the death of Rameses a new Dynasty, the Twentieth, had taken over.

This Dynasty produced one more great ruler in the person of Rameses III. Egypt was now hard pressed by foreign invaders both by land and sea but Rameses prevailed and his last years were apparently years of peace during which, as we shall see at Medinet Habu, some remarkable building took place. But on the other—priestly—front the reign was in decline. Now begins the final and fatal triumph of the priests of Amun. Some idea of their power may be gleaned from the recorded facts that in the reign of Rameses III more than two-thirds of the landed property of the priests of Egypt belonged to them, three-quarters of the religious donations of the Pharaohs went to them and that of 113,433 slaves taken no fewer than 86,486 were presented to them. Eight succeeding Pharaohs all called Rameses appear to have fallen increasingly under the priestly power and the final indignity came when the royal throne was actually usurped by a high priest with the name of Herihor.

We have now reached the date 1100 BC. In the centuries that followed, the power of the states and empires that surrounded Egypt tended to increase while Egypt itself was periodically a prey to divisions that left it less and less capable of making head against the foreigners. Six more Dynasties are identified before the country succumbed finally to foreign conquest but if any of them achieved greatness they have left few records of it. The almost immediate result of the elevation of Herihor was that the country fell to pieces; a new Dynasty arose in the Delta with its capital at Tanis; and the Egyptian domination in Nubia and Palestine was quickly lost. A family of Libyan origin is said to have founded the Twenty-Second Dynasty with a capital also in the Delta, but now at Bubastis instead of Tanis. Among its rulers was Sheshouk or Shishak who appears in the Bible as the Egyptian Pharaoh who captured Jerusalem and plundered the temple of Solomon, a minor triumph which we will find recorded in an inscription at Karnak. Under his successors the country became sub-divided into principalities which are dignified with the name of the Twenty-Third Dynasty. A new and formidable adversary now appeared in the person of Piankhi, king of Ethiopia who conquered Upper Egypt; Lower Egypt remained for a time under the rule of Bocchoris of the Twenty-Fourth Dynasty but he too was overthrown by an Ethiopian monarch and the whole country became subject to Ethiopian rule. The Twenty-Fifth Dynasty was an Ethiopian Dynasty.

The new menace to Egypt was now the great Assyrian Empire centred on the Mesopotamian Babylon. Three Pharaohs of the new Dynasty combined with the Palestinians against the new enemy, but in 670 BC the Pharaoh Tahaska was defeated, Memphis was laid waste and the whole country came temporarily under Assyrian rule. His son was able to take advantage of the absence of the Assyrian forces in other theatres to win back independence and Egypt again enjoyed a brief prosperity. The last truly independent Dynasty, the Twenty-Sixth, was founded by Psammeticus I who started a small dynasty at Sais in the Delta and was followed by five successors. The wars with Assyria continued with fluctuating fortune, while a new influence on Egypt made itself felt with the development of Greek power in the Mediterranean. It was at this period that the town of Naucratis was established in the Delta for the exclusive use of Greek colonists.

But Egypt, Greece and Assyria were alike threatened in the sixth century BC with a new and formidable power in the shape of the Persian Empire. In 538 BC the Persian monarch Cyrus captured Babylon and destroyed the Assyrian Empire; thirteen years later he invaded Egypt. The last independent Egyptian Pharaoh Psammeticus III was defeated at Pelusium and Egypt became a Persian province.

After all the convulsions we have witnessed through thousands of years this was a new experience for the country. We have seen Egypt ruled by native dynasties; we have seen it ruled as an independent country by dynasties whose origin was foreign; we have seen it temporarily conquered by foreign powers. Now Egypt was to suffer a new experience, the first of several, as a distant province of a great empire ruled from hundreds of miles away by rulers who had hardly heard of Egypt. The Persian Empire has been handed down to us principally by very hostile writers, the Greek historians. Greece which was on the fringe of the Empire alternately hated it and feared it and trafficked with it in furtherance of intestine wars. But the Persian Empire, as those who have seen Persepolis can imagine, was an impressive political achievement. The Persian king who conquered Egypt was Cambyses; his son Darius took the conquest seriously and notwithstanding the distance from his capital gave detailed attention to its administration and economy.

It is difficult to judge at this distance of time whether his concern was the welfare of the Egyptian people or the power of his own empire. He is said to have completed the canal from the Nile to the Red Sea, to have built a shrine in the oasis of Khargali, to have confiscated the enormous revenues of the ancient Egyptian temples. How far this made him popular we cannot judge nor how far these measures were beneficial to the people. What is recorded is that both under Darius and his successors numerous revolts of the Egyptians occurred. We should not perhaps take these completely at face value as evidence of anti-Persian feeling; the Greek world was now arrayed against the Persian; and it was doubtless as a result of successive Greek intrigues that the Egyptians were persuaded to collaborate against their new tyrants. The Greek victory at Marathon inspired a revolt which temporarily expelled the Persians altogether but the victory was fleeting and it was not until the end of the fifth century BC that the Egyptians regained a last independence.

It was during the fifth century, in the reign of the Persian king Artaxerxes, that the Greek historian Herodotus paid his famous visit. It says something for the Persian rule that a native from a country by no means friendly to the Persians should not merely have been admitted to the country but should have found himself free, as he apparently did, to traverse it without let or hindrance, make friends with the natives and record his impressions for the benefit of his own compatriots. Herodotus is one of the most entertaining of Greek writers but he was clearly conscious of this fact and anxious both to be listened to and to be read. It is the misfortune of posterity that reading his descriptions we have to separate what was his own accurate observation from stories that are clearly tall. Yet his verdict on the Egyptians, in the last century before Egypt became a Mediterranean nation and part of Greek civilisation, is not without interest. 'As the Egyptians have a climate peculiar to themselves, and their river is different in nature from all other rivers, so they have made all their customs and laws of a

kind contrary for the most part to those of other men. Among
them, the women buy and sell, the men bide at home and weave…
men carry burdens on their heads, women on their shoulders.
Women make water standing, men sitting. They relieve nature
indoors, and eat out of doors in the streets, giving the reason that
things unseemly but necessary should be done in secret, things
not unseemly should be done openly. No woman is dedicated to
the service of any god or goddess; men are dedicated to all deities
male and female. Sons are not compelled against their will to
support their parents, but daughters must do so though they be
unwilling. Everywhere else, priests of the gods wear their hair
long; in Egypt they are shaven…. The Egyptians are the only
people who keep animals with them in the house…. They knead
dough with their feet and gather mud and dung with their hands….
Every man has two garments, every woman only one…. The
Greeks write and calculate by moving the hand from left to right;
the Egyptians do contrariwise…. They are beyond measure
religious, more than any other nation….' And so on. It is Herodotus
also who gives us the most vivid impression of the annual inundation of the Nile and of the appearance of the Delta as it must
have been every season until the nineteenth century: 'When the
Nile overflows the land, the towns alone are seen high and dry
above the water, very like to the islands in the Aegean Sea. These
alone stand out, the rest of Egypt being a sheet of water. So when
this happens folk are ferried not, as is their wont, in the course
of the stream, but clean over the plain. From Naucratis to Memphis
the boat going upwards passes close by the pyramids
themselves….'

The Persian monarchs are chronicled by Manetho as the Twenty-
Seventh Dynasty. Their rule did not finish until the historic year
323 BC but in the meantime the Egyptians did successfully revolt
and established three final short Dynasties of their own. The first
ruler of the Thirtieth Dynasty effectively re-united the country
and we shall find him as a builder on a considerable scale in Upper
Egypt notably at Karnak and Philae. But his successors failed to
maintain themselves against the Persians; the Persian power was
re-established in 341 BC and Egypt might have remained a Persian
province indefinitely but for a new and totally unexpected turn of
history. This was the emergence of Alexander.

Alexander succeeded as a relatively young man to the kingship
of the comparatively small country of Macedonia in Northern
Greece. He made it his life's ambition to destroy the Persian Empire

and by a series of miraculous campaigns he succeeded. The news was apparently received with enthusiasm in Egypt and he was eagerly summoned as a deliverer. He appeared and took possession of the country.

Happy is the country that has no history. Henceforward the history of Egypt for a thousand years is the history of Alexandria and there we shall pursue it. The thousand years covered not only Alexander himself, but also the Greek dynasty of the Ptolemies, the Roman Emperors and the Rule of Byzantium. What happened during this long period to Egypt itself? It is difficult to say, but it is possible to hope that it was better governed than at most other periods of its history. It was now, first a province, then an independent state, then under the Romans and Byzantines again a province. We shall when we visit Upper Egypt see that both Ptolemies and Roman Emperors took a periodical interest in its welfare. But so far as real history is concerned, Egypt slept.

3 ALEXANDRIA

Alexandria has become in recent years a city for the arm-chair traveller. For a whole century, from the 1840s to the 1940s, it was the first Egyptian landfall, both for the traveller to Egypt and for the traveller to India. The curiously named 'Overland Route' came into fashion. Disembarking at Alexandria, the Indian traveller would proceed, in early days by canal, later by railway, to Cairo and would then drive in a horse-drawn vehicle across the desert to Suez to take ship for Bombay. All this was made possible by the resurgence of Alexandria and indeed of Egypt by the extraordinary tyrant Mehemet Ali.

With the opening of the Suez Canal Alexandria lost its monopoly. Port Said became a rival port and Indian travellers preferred to do the whole journey by sea. But it is the aeroplane that has almost wiped the city off the tourist map. Travellers to India no longer travel by sea at all and visitors to Egypt land at Cairo airport.

All this must be a sadness for the historically-minded. For in all the world there can be few cities which have had a more splendid past. The nineteenth-century resurgence, wonderful though it was, was a pale shadow of the ancient city. There was a time, about two hundred years before Christ, when Alexandria was the most splendid city in the world.

It was the creation, as its name implied, of Alexander the Great. The 25-year-old King had defeated the Persian monarch and had occupied Egypt, then one of the provinces of the Persian Empire. Ancient Egypt had been centred on the Nile Valley; Persian Egypt had been centred far to the East on the two sides of the Persian gulf; now for the first time in history Egypt had become a province of a Mediterranean power. It was necessary that it should have a Mediterranean capital.

The chosen site was remarkable. On the western edge of the Delta, on the eastern tip of the desert, it stretched itself along the coast upon a strip of limestone bounded on the south by a lake or canal and on the north by the sea.

The young conqueror did not stay to see it built though

apparently he dictated the plan. Astonishingly the plan went forward. Eight years later, without ever having revisited his city, Alexander died. His general Ptolemy made himself the master of his Egypt and his first care was to secure Alexander's body. Brought to Egypt and first to Memphis, it was decided finally and rightly that he should be entombed in the new city. A splendid burial chamber known as the Soma was erected in the city centre; it has vanished now without trace.

The city is said to have been build in transatlantic style. Straight streets crossing at right angles dictated the plan. But the streets were not as transatlantic streets. Certainly the two main streets, intersecting near Alexander's tomb, must have been unlike the streets of any other city; 200 feet wide and lined with colonnades.

Lying off the sea front, and at no great distance was a long and narrow island represented in the modern city by the northern extension which terminates in the west at the Palace of Ras-et-tin and in the east at Fort Kait Bey. The Ptolemies built a causeway to connect this island with the city; the accumulations of centuries have widened the causeway; and it is now that area that forms the northern quarter of the town. Where Fort Kait Bey now stands, the Ptolemies built the most famous building of Alexandria. This was the Pharos.

The Pharos was one of the Seven Wonders of the World. Yet its origin was primarily practical; on this low-lying coast it was essential that ships should have good warning; the great height of the lighthouse—it rose to 400 feet—was additionally to command both harbours of the city and to communicate with other light-houses down the length of the North African coast. The Pharos was still erect at the time of the Arab conquest; it is not known for certain how long it survived. Certainly by the end of the Middle Ages it was in ruins; it was then that one of the Mameluke caliphs built on its site the fort that we now know as Kait Bey.

The result of building the causeway to the Pharos island was to divide the foreshore into two harbours—the Western Harbour and the Eastern Harbour. These still survive today. A small promontory at the south-eastern edge of the Eastern Harbour is thought to be the site of the Palace of the Ptolemies. (We write of the Ptolemies. This was the family and dynasty which derived from the original general of Alexander and ruled in Egypt, with vicissitudes some of which we shall follow, until the ultimate climax and the last of their line, the famous Cleopatra).

South of the palace of the Ptolemies was Alexandria's second most famous building, the Mouseion. This was the great intellectual centre, founded by the first of the Ptolemies and including among its wonders the famous Library reputed in its heyday to have possessed 500,000 volumes. It was the great power-house of Alexandrian scholarship; a scholarship which subjected the Greek language and Greek literature to a detailed research and examination it had never had before, which invented Greek grammar and which systematized the great tradition of critical analysis of the Classical texts. The sciences as well as literature made the fame of the Mouseion; gemoetry was invented by Euclid, geography and astronomy were scientifically developed by Eratosthenes; and medicine became a branch of knowledge rather than a cult.

The library is said to have been burnt in the war which broke out in the city at the time of Julius Caesar's invasion. Cleopatra launched a new foundation, making a fresh collection which she attached to the Serapeum. The Serapeum and the Caesareum were the two great temples of the city. The Serapeum stood on the slight hill which still today is the principal natural feature of Alexandria and which is marked by the solitary survival of antiquity known as Pompey's Pillar. The Caesareum stood probably near the modern sea front of the Eastern harbour; begun by Cleopatra in honour of Mark Anthony, it was finished by Augustus and dedicated in his own honour; as described by a later writer it was both high and large, full of treasures and extended into galleries, courts and halls as glorious as expense and art could make them. To adorn the exterior there were brought in the year 13 BC the two obelisks which in the nineteenth century were removed respectively to London and New York.

Not the least of the wonders of ancient Alexandria was the so-called Soma, the tomb of Alexander the Great and of the dynasty of the Ptolemies which stood, as already mentioned, in the very centre of the city. How long this survived cannot now be said.

The remarkable thing about so great a city is, that so far as visible remains are concerned, it has almost vanished without trace. In modern times some excavations have been attempted in the southern sector and various foundations have been cleared. If the same thing could be done over the whole city, doubtless the original plan would be visible. But still there would be nothing appreciable above ground level. The only real monument of antiquity is the so-called Pompey's Pillar, actually unconnected with Pompey and no part of the Ptolemaic city; it is of red granite from Assuan and was apparently erected by a Roman prefect in honour of the

Emperor Diocletian.

The first Alexandria from the time of its foundation had a history of nearly a thousand years, successively Ptolemaic, Roman and Byzantine. The first Ptolemy, sometimes called Soter, founded a dynasty which began by being distinguished and then became degenerate. It was probably his successor, sometimes called Philadelphus, who built the Pharos to the design of the great architect Sostratus. Both first and second Ptolemies engaged extensively in foreign wars. Expeditions were launched to Greece and Cyprus; Palestine was constantly fought over with the Seleucid dynasty which had inherited Alexander's Asiatic dominions; naval control was secured over the Eastern Mediterranean. The strain on the economy of Egypt of these wars so remote from the people of the Nile must have been considerable; nevertheless in military and imperial terms the effort paid off and by the time of the third Ptolemy not only the coast of Greece but large areas of the Asiatic mainland were under Egyptian rule.

It was under the fourth and fifth Ptolemies that decline set in. Greece and Asia were lost and two developments, pregnant with future history, occurred. First, the Romans intervened in the Eastern Mediterranean; secondly, a new name entered the Ptolemaic dynasty when the fifth Ptolemy accepted as a bride the daughter of the Seleucid monarch called Cleopatra. Henceforward there was a Cleopatra in each generation; henceforward Egypt existed increasingly under the shadow of Rome.

With the sixth Ptolemy, called Philometer, the dynasty began a long nose-dive to disaster. It was arranged that he should marry his sister and rule jointly with his brother Euergetes, the seventh Ptolemy. This unpromising set-up did not long endure; Philometer died in battle; his infant son was killed; and Euergetes seized both his wife and his throne. From this last union were descended the three last generations of the Ptolemies. The final generation consisted of two more Ptolemies and three sisters one of whom was the celebrated Cleopatra.

Cleopatra has come down to us as one of the great heroines of history, a creature of love and romance, of mystery and heroism, whose ultimate end was a tragic culmination born of the failures of others and her own misfortune. It is possible to formulate a very different view. It is possible to depict her as a cold-blooded schemer, unscrupulous and ruthless, whose life was dominated by an ambition that in truth was boundless; to be the empress and effective ruler of the whole civilised world. Her life was passed against the background of the last great power struggles within the Roman Republic, Caesar against Pompey, Octavian against Anthony; and it was her purpose and to some extent her achievement to extract from these the maximum personal power to herself.

Her extraordinary adventures began when, having been proclaimed sovereign jointly with her brother, she fled to Syria and raised an army to dethrone him. At this point arrived Julius Caesar in pursuit of Pompey; Cleopatra had herself smuggled into his presence at Alexandria and soon persuaded him to become her lover. Their extraordinary proceedings are well recorded by Bernard Shaw in his play *Caesar and Cleopatra;* Caesar stayed some months in the city, sustained a siege in one of its buildings, fought a civil war with the Alexandrians and finally executed Cleopatra's brother, thus leaving her sole queen of Egypt. In the year 47 BC she bore him a son Caesarion. Cleopatra's triumph was complete when on his return to Rome she followed him and set herself up there in state as his acknowledged mistress. All seemed set for an ultimate dénouement in which Caesar would be recognised as permanent dictator and he and Cleopatra would be established as rulers of the Mediterranean world.

But Caesar's assassination supervened, and she returned to Egypt. The Roman world was divided, the West to Octavian, the East to Mark Anthony; and Anthony summoned her to meet him in Asia Minor. She arrived in full splendour and Anthony became her slave. It was her second triumph. They spent a winter together; she bore him two children; she persuaded him to execute her sister; a few years later he formally abandoned his lawful wife and came to live permanently with her. The old Egyptian conquests were restored; honours were heaped upon her children; effectively she was now co-ruler of half the Roman world.

Prospects darkened when increasingly Anthony and Octavian failed to agree and it came to open war. Queens do not usually go into battle; nevertheless it seems clear that Cleopatra led the Egyptian navy to the sea battle of Actium. But at the crisis of the battle her nerve failed her and her contingent was withdrawn. Anthony followed her; the battle was lost; they got back to Alexandria but they were now defenceless against Octavian. The rest of the story has been told by Shakespeare; Anthony, believing she was dead, himself committed suicide and died in her arms. Still she did not give up hope; she might have a third triumph with Octavian. But Octavian was too cold a fish. When it was plain that he would not yield to her, she too committed suicide, it is said by the medium of an asp.

At this point the question may be asked: what has all this to do with Egypt? And the answer must be: very little. For the astonishing characteristic of Alexandria, occupying the best site in Egypt, is that until modern times it had led a life apart. The Ptolemies were Greeks and the Alexandrians in the main were Hellenes; they had little in common with the mass of the Egyptians and led a largely self-contained life, supported obviously by the taxes levied on the Egyptian natives but spiritually and economically living in an almost private world of their own. The records are scanty and the evidence is slight; one great revolt is recorded which appears to have resulted in the destruction of Memphis; otherwise the Egyptians appear to have accepted placidly the new dynasty as in past ages they had accepted Pharaohs, Hyskos and Persians. And the Ptolemies evidently pandered to their subjects; the ancient traditional gods were accorded their accustomed right and worship; and when we reach Upper Egypt we shall find great temples of the Ptolemies replete with the religious paraphernalia of former ages, built on the traditional Pharaonic plan and making only the smallest obeisance to the architectural tradition of Classical Greece. And this tradition was to continue through the succeeding phase of Alexandrian history, when Egypt, no longer now a kingdom, carried on as a principal province of the Roman Empire.

To Octavian, shortly to be re-named Augustus, fell the task of restoring order to the distracted Roman world; and not the least of his pre-occupations was Egypt. It is the modern fashion to decry Augustus, to depict him as a mediocrity, hard-faced and unimaginative, living on the reputation and achievements of forbears and contemporaries more able and more civilised than himself. He was, none the less, the effective restorer of the Roman World and the effective restorer of Egypt and he established for the Egyptians a settled status which was to see their country through the next three hundred years. The Mediterranean world was divided into provinces and Egypt was made a province, but a province of a very special kind. It was established as a sort of preserve of the Emperors. How much the personal vanity of Augustus entered into this, how much was due to the special character of the country, so unlike the rest of the Mediterranean world, we do not know. It is even possible that its special status was decided by crudely practical considerations. Egypt under the Ptolemies had become a great grain-exporting country and, with the decline of Italian agriculture, wheat imports had become a critically important factor in the task of feeding and controlling the huge city popoulation of Rome. Alexandria, so famous for its philosophy and its art, was perhaps more important in imperial eyes as the great grain-exporting port.

In any event a special regime was established for the country. It was governed, not like the other provinces by a senator, but by a prefect of equestrian rank; senators and other official figures were forbidden to visit it without special imperial permission; it became in some degree the emperor's private domain. And in it and through the centuries the emperors continued in the main the Ptolemaic tradition. They now were the latest successors of the Pharaohs; they received the long customary honours from priests and cities; they continued the tradition of building the great temples in the ancient manner of the realm.

Also, following the Ptolemies, they maintained Alexandria as the national capital. It was Augustus who transported thither the two obelisks eventually removed to London and New York. Diodorus, a contemporary writer, has left statistics suggesting that in the time of Augustus the city had a population of some half million souls. Though there was an Egyptian element, the population preponderantly still was Greek; a significant minority occasionally heard of in history was provided by the Jews. The Roman period seems to have been both prosperous and happy. Eastern ventures were pioneered by mariners and bankers and Alexandria, in addition to its grain exports, became a centre of entrepôt trade from countries as far away as India and Ceylon. Unappreciative of their good fortune, the Alexandrians nevertheless established their reputation as some of the biggest trouble-makers of the Empire; hostilities between Greeks and Jews were always simmering; and in one riot some fifty years after Augustus' death it is said that 50,000 Jews were killed. There was a serious repetition in the reign of Trajan. In the following century the Greeks disgraced themselves by a furious riot against the Emperor Caracalla which he repaid by a wholesale massacre.

These discreditable episodes were soon forgotten in a new phase of Alexandrian history resulting from the emergence of Christianity. As the second city of the Empire, Alexandria became the seat of the second of the Christian Patriarchs exercising jurisdiction over a vast area of Eastern Christianity. Unfortunately it became the focus also for those tremendous disputes and discussions about doctrine which have ever been the foible of the Eastern Christians.

Already in the second century after Christ the Gnostics had been active; in the following hundred years Orthodoxy was proclaimed first by Clement, later by Origen; later still Egyptian Christianity was dominated by the tremendous figure of Athanasius. Meanwhile a fundamental transformation had been effected in the imperial sphere; the Emperor Constantine declared himself a convert to the new religion and simultaneously prepared the way for that division of the Empire that was destined to divide both the imperial power and religion into the separate spheres of East and West. No less important, he founded Constantinople and established it as the Eastern capital.

Alexandria found itself thus demoted from the position which it had enjoyed for six hundred years as the capital of the Eastern Mediterranean. Henceforward she continued as the second city of the Eastern Empire which from the ancient name of its new capital is known to us as Byzantine. A critical step in the history of Alexandria and Egypt was taken by the Byzantine Emperor Theo-dosius when he ordered the closure of the ancient Egyptian temples; this marked the final triumph of monotheistic religion over the traditional gods of Egypt.

But the new religion failed increasingly to achieve agreement among its adherents upon the intricate questions of doctrine. Historians from Gibbon onwards have amused themselves and their readers with tracing the semantics of the competing schools and sects. After the disappearance of Gnosticism, Arianism took the stage and the thunders of Athanasius, now enshrined in the Nicene Creed, were needed to extinguish it. But a more serious development was Monophysism. This concerned the nature of Christ, specifically asserting that Christ did not have two natures, divine and human, but one nature in which the human was absorbed by the divine. The passions which this controversy provoked became a public danger to the Emperors who increasingly concerned themselves with securing ecclesiastical peace. A great Council was summoned at Chalcedon but here the fatal step was taken of condemning the doctrine of Monophysism and laying down what is still the Christian orthodox view, that Christ had two natures unmixed and unchangeable. The effect in Egypt was disastrous. Monophysism had taken an almost universal hold; the country slid into religious munity; and the Orthodox Patriarch of Alexandria lost almost all his followers. Astonishingly, after fifteen centuries, this situation remains. The Copts, as the Egyptian Christians came to be called, have remained permanently out of communion with the rest of Christianity.

One last desperate effort to retrieve this situation was destined to be made. The Byzantine Empire in the seventh century AD was enduring increasing strains which made more and more important the restoration and preservation of a united people. The Emperor Heraclius, engaged in a desperate struggle with the Persian Empire, resolved on a final initiative to bring his contending subjects together. A religious compromise was proposed, a general agreement to accept that while Christ might have two Natures, he had only one Will. The attempt was a disaster; it failed as a compromise and survived only as a heresy easily accepted and still proclaimed under the name of Monothelism by the Christians of the Lebanon. Meanwhile a greater threat than the Persian Empire was menacing Heraclius. An obscure prophet called Mohammed preached his doctrines in Arabia; his followers sallied forth in conquest; and soon an Arab army reached Alexandria. And now, so violent were the resentments against the Byzantine emperors, that the Alexandrians were simply not prepared to fight. Alexandria surrendered and the whole of Egypt. It was the end of a civilisation and of a city.

For it meant that Egypt had finished its thousand-year role as a Mediterranean state and that Alexandria had finished its thousand-year role as the national capital. Though the Arabs did not wholly neglect it, they fixed their new capital at Cairo and through the years and centuries Alexandria contracted and declined. Its first Arab conqueror described it as a city of 4,000 palaces and 4,000 baths. When after another twelve centuries it again emerged into history, it was a place of barely 4,000 inhabitants. The Pharos had fallen down, the other great buildings of antiquity mouldered or were destroyed. With one exception the Arabs built only walls. The exception was the Fort of Kait Bey built in the fifteenth century by a Mameluke Sultan as a protection against the threatening Turks. The effort was futile; the Turks conquered; and the city continued in decline.

Alexandria provided a small prelude and a small epitaph to the expedition of Napoleon Bonaparte in the years 1798 and 1801. The French landed eight miles to the west at Marabout and immediately marched on the city. Pompey's Pillar, then outside the walls, became their headquarters for several days. The city soon was taken; Bonaparte's only urge was to leave it as soon as possible and march on Cairo. Shortly afterwards the French battle fleet, which had escorted him from Toulon, was annihilated at

Aboukir Bay by Nelson in the famous Battle of the Nile. A year later the Turks landed an invading army at the same place. Swiftly moving a large force from Cairo, Bonaparte attacked them and drove them into the sea. Among the fugitives who managed to save themselves by clambering on a boat was a young officer called Mehemet Ali destined to play a major part in the later destiny of Egypt and Alexandria. A month later, with a few companions and in greatest secrecy, Bonaparte decamped to France.

The epilogue came in 1801 when the deserted French army had to face an English invading force disembarking once again at Aboukir Bay. The French lost the battle and retreated to Alexandria. It was then that the British commander gave the order, so pregnant for the future of the city, to cut through a narrow isthmus and let the Mediterranean into Lake Mariout, thus isolating the French. After two months they capitulated and after another month they were shipped back to France. Alexandria relapsed into its slum-like and obscure self.

Some eighteen years later it was suddenly projected into a new destiny. Mehemet Ali, now pasha of Egypt, fixed upon it as the key point of a newly-to-be-developed Egypt. By forced labour he had a canal built—the Mahmoudieh—to connect it with the Nile. At once its maritime trade boomed. The harbours were re-activated, locks and arsenals were built, a fleet was added; all this required the supporting presence of a new and re-planned city. The new Alexandria, alas, was no equal of the Ancient. Egypt was poor, Mehemet Ali was ill-educated, he threw himself deliberately on the help of the European entrepreneurs. A confused and ill-organised rush for sites began. Only one real stand for civic dignity was made, the Place des Consuls, later called Place Mehemet Ali and finally re-christened Midan-el-Tahrir or Liberation Square. This is ornamented with a statue of the pasha, one of the few modern works of art in Alexandria of some distinction.

Mehemet Ali had made the city his capital and built his royal palace. This was the so-called Ras-et-Tin built at the western tip of the Pharos island and a building of some note. Formerly open to tourists (a privilege apparently now denied), it displayed an interior no longer contemporary with its founder but redolent rather of the extravagant Ismail. This and Fort Kait Bey, which still survives at the other end of the island on the actual site of the Pharos, form the principal human scenery of the seaward side of the town. The Fort, thanks to its conversion into a small naval museum, may now be visited and the credulous antiquary may find around its northern base some rudimentary relics of its famous predecessor.

In material terms the new Alexandria was a success story. Its growth was upon a transatlantic scale. Mehemet Ali's reliance upon Europeans resulted deliberately in a huge influx of Europeans— French, Italians, Greeks—and in a sequence of modern developments which were mainly French-inspired. The city, if it did not recover its ancient distinction, recovered its ancient character as the greatest of the Levant. But once again, though less than under the Ptolemies, it acquired a life divorced from Egypt as a whole. The reaction came in the later twentieth century. Arab nationalist uprisings, civic riots, made it clear to the Europeans that they were no longer welcome. A vast and sustained emigration began. Simultaneously the French names disappeared from the streets and buildings. Alexandria became, as never before, an Arab city. Nor was the emigration noticed. Individual disasters, it was true, disfigured the city and its surroundings; palaces decayed, villas collapsed, gardens became jungles. But the population increased; the guide books could no longer keep up with the statistics; half a million, one million, two million inhabited the city and its environs. And its streets and buildings acquired new Arabic names.

The city centre has shifted eastwards from the Place Mehemet Ali. The Salah-Salan Street (once Rue Cherif) leading from it remains, it is true, the centre of the fashionable shops and important offices; but the nerve centre is now to the north or north-east in the small square called Saad Zagloul. Here is a statue of the later hero; and hence depart some of the city's busiest streets. It is without any intention of disparaging a great and famous city to say that few of these deserve much of the visitor's time. In the city itself the principal remaining objects of interest are the excavations and the museum.

The principal excavations are three in number; the Anfonchi; the Kom-ed-dik; and the Kom-el-Chogafa. The Anfonchi is an ancient necropolis close to the Ras-et-Tin; it is a series of underground tombs of which two are of some importance; their interest is in their decorations which are identifiably of mid-Ptolemaic period. Rather more impressive are the tombs of Kom-el-Chogafa, close to Pompey's column, which appear to cover also the Roman and the Christian periods. Kom-ed-dik, a little south of the Saad Zagloul square, is a comparatively recent excavation centred round a Roman theatre, adjoined by what appears to have been a vast Roman bathing establishment.

But the best of ancient Alexandria is in the museum. For anyone who has not seen an Egyptian museum this would make an agreeable introduction; almost all the phases of Egypt are represented and almost all forms of Egyptian art; sculptures, figures, portrait busts; mummies and small objects of art; mosaics, ceramics, bronzes; sphinxes, coins, gold and marble; there is no lack of variety. But for those who have seen all this before (or who are about to see it in Cairo) the outstanding interest of this museum is specifically Alexandrian, that is to say, the period of the Ptolemies, of the Romans and of the Christian Byzantines. And if one had to choose one collection, it would surely be the small statuettes in earthenware or porcelain, known from their resemblance to a collection from mainland Greece as the Tanagra figures. Here one can savour the carefree life of the subjects of the Ptolemies, richly dressed ladies, children, musicians, dancers and favourite animals, most of them still richly coloured.

What else is there to see in Alexandria? In the absence of Alexander's tomb there are the tombs of some of Mehemet Ali's family including his grandson Said, enclosed in the small mosque of Nebi Daniel. There are the innumerable churches and places of worship of both Moslems and Christians; for the latter, drawn here by Mehemet Ali, reproduced in brick and stone a formidable variety of faiths and sectaries not unworthy of the controversies of Early Christian times. There is the former Cotton Exchange, source and foundation of the nineteenth-century city, later transformed into the Arab Socialist Union. There is the railway station, there is the town hall....

But it is better to break away from this to see the beaches. Alexandria must be one of the world's longest cities and gives the appearance of projecting itself almost indefinitely to east and west. To the west, after threading the industrial districts of Gabbari and Mex, the road and railway cross Lake Mariout and reach the beach of Agami. The chief objects of tourist interest in this area are Abusir and the City of St Menas. Abusir is the site of the ancient Taposiris Magna; there is not much left except the emplacement of the ancient Egyptian temple; but the views of arable, desert and sea suggest it as a suitable destination for a picnic. The city of St Menas has a portentous historical background originating with the third-century saint who became a regular cult for the Egyptian Christians. A whole city arose in the desert some miles inland; and the Byzantine Emperor Arcadius erected in his honour a great Basilica the design of which is still clearly seen.

But the fashionable projection of Alexandria has always been to the East. Here along the coast we come to Ramlah, now in effect part of the city but once an elegant European suburb; thence to Montazah, and finally to Aboukir Bay. Montazah is worth visiting as an example of the burdens which the twentieth-century Egyptians have had to bear. Situated in an enormous park, it is a creation of the last sovereigns of Mehemet Ali's dynasty, King Fuad and King Farouk. Clearly no expense was spared; nothing was wanting except taste. The interior is curious for its somewhat jejune presentation; one gets the feeling that nothing has been altered for the tourist and that it is as Farouk left it. Aboukir Bay, further on, has natural beauties, historical memories and the ruins of the ancient city of Canopus; and if Alexandria has an end, this is it. Fifteen miles of beaches fringe this coast, but it would be a bold prophecy as to what sort of welcome they will give the tourist in years to come. Some of them, one fears, will be better considered from the viewpoint with which this chapter started, the arm-chair.

4 HISTORICAL — FROM AMR TO SADAT

It is seldom easy to re-create the state of mind of peoples of past ages. It is astonishingly difficult to re-create the state of mind of the Egyptians in the year of Our Lord 641, the year of the Moslem conquest.

Egypt had been for nearly a thousand years part of the civilisation of the Mediterranean world. For three hundred years it had been a Christian country and its ancient traditional gods had been proscribed and overthrown. This was the first triumph of monotheism; in 641 AD Egypt was facing the challenge of a second monotheism, the religion of Mahomet. The enemy was, literally, at the gates.

The country had undergone a similar experience with Alexander the Great. But its inhabitants had had a long foretaste of what the rule of Alexander might mean. Long-established relations with the Greeks — often in alliance with them against the Persian Empire — must have satisfied the Egyptians that the rule of a Greek conqueror would not be incompatible with the maintenance of their own institutions and their own religion. And so it proved.

Did the Egyptians have the same confidence in regard to the invading armies of Islam? They can have had but slender contacts with the inhabitants of Arabia whence principally the Moslems came. They can have known but little of the beliefs and character of the new religion. Yet the historical evidence suggests that these new invaders, like Alexander the Great, were not merely accepted but welcomed. Alexandria, it is true, was long defended by the Byzantines, but the fortress of Babylon near the modern Cairo which was in truth the key of Egypt was peacefully handed over and apparently through the intervention of the Christian patriarch himself.

Our knowledge of what lay in store for the Egyptians in the ages that followed provokes the question: how could such a decision have been taken? And the only answer can be: as a result of the astonishing virulence of the religious disputes which divided the Egyptian Christians from their Christian rulers in Constantinople.

It is arguable that in the face of the Islamic armies the Egyptians had no choice. But the Byzantines only a few years previously had thrown out of Egypt some Parthian invaders. The Byzantine Emperors in the later seventh century successfully resisted far more serious challenges from the Arab armies. The conclusion must be that had the Egyptian Christians supported their Christian rulers the Moslem conquest would not have happened. They preferred not to do so.

What it is impossible to know is how far these developments involved the Egyptian people as a whole. Was Egyptian Christianity a matter of life and death to the peasant toiling on his strip by the Nile in Upper Egypt? Was it a mass-movement raising the passions of the mob in Alexandria and Memphis? Or was it the preserve of a small religious class, dispensing their authority indeed to the Egyptian people, but reserving to themselves the great issues on which the future of their country and their religion would turn? To us, with the advantage of hindsight, the consequences seem predictable and obvious. Islam was, from the first, a proselytising religion. The Mohammedan conquerors, it is true, early evolved a system of government of non-Moslem subjects under which their religious leaders would continue to hold some sway and their principal obligation would be to pay tribute to their Moslem masters. But Islam was not only a proselytising religion, it was a religion peculiarly characterised by outbreaks of fanaticism. It would seem inevitable, as in fact happened through the centuries, that sooner or later the subject people would find itself faced with implacable alternatives that must result for many of them in the abandonment of their traditional faith. At no time can there have been any great infusion of new Arab inhabitants into the country. Yet if we leap the centuries and look at the present day, we find that the country which in 641 AD was 100% Christian is now 90% Moslem. And the evidence is that the process of conversion started almost immediately.

The original inspiration of Islam, as of Christianity, was unity in the faith. But in the manner of their propagation there is no comparison between the two religions. There has never been an explosion like Islam, an explosion religious, political and military. Within half a century of Mahommed's Hegira the Moslems had conquered half the known world. Egypt was one of their comparatively early conquests. But so great a territorial expansion was fatal to the concept of unity. And a fatal breach at any early date marred the conception of the unitary Caliphate. The adherents of Ali, the Prophet's son-in-law, married to the Prophet's daughter Fatima, claimed that the Caliphate was hereditary in his family; the rest of Islam claimed it was elective. The followers of Ali—the so-called Shia Moslems or Fatimids—were labelled the heretics; the rest of Islam—the so-called Sunni—became the orthodox. Egypt at an early date was involved in their contests but by the year 660 AD the orthodox had prevailed. Similarly, in the broader world, the Shiites had been worsted by the Orthodox who established the first great Moslem dynasty, the Umaiyads, with their capital at Damascus. For a hundred years they ruled Egypt and they seem to have taken trouble with this rule. It was now that the Arab administration was developed; it was doubtless now also that the first pressures were applied that began the drift of the Egyptian people from Christianity to Islam.

Surprisingly this great dynasty has left no Egyptian monuments. The mosque of Amr, in a much rebuilt state, survives at Cairo to remind us of the general who conquered Babylon. But there is nothing comparable to the great mosque of Damascus.

The dynasties of Islam were no more permanent than the dynasties of Ancient Egypt, and there has, alas, been no Manetho to give them a numerical classification. Like the dynasties of Ancient Egypt, they sometimes followed the line of a single family, sometimes changed violently from usurper to usurper; and the student who follows the vicissitudes of the centuries is sometimes unhappily aware of eras comparable to those 'Intermediate Periods' which throw such dark shadows into the history of Ancient Egypt.

The Umaiyads of Damascus were displaced by the Abassids of Baghdad, a great and splendid dynasty which included the famous Harun-al-Raschid, and Egypt was ruled by their frequently changing governors. In the ninth century an enterprising governor Ibn-Tulun broke free from his distant sovereigns and established a brief dynasty of his own. This was followed by another independent dynasty the Ikchidites, but the country was weakened by dissensions and succumbed to invaders who dramatically transformed the character of Egyptian government.

The Abassids, like the Umaiyads, have left no great relics in Egypt. But by contrast the usurper Ibn-Tulun is one of the most dramatic names in Cairo. He laid out a whole new city north of the older settlements and immortalised himself by building the gigantic congregational mosque which still bears his name.

A major revolution in this history of Islamic Egypt occurred in the year 969 AD as a result of the conquest of the country by a

Shia dynasty, the so-called Fatimids. Unlike all other conquerors
of Egypt the Fatimids came from the West where they had built
up a great territorial dominion comprising all the coasts of North
Africa. Once again it is impossible to re-create the state of mind of
the Egyptians at this moment, suddenly subjected to heretics. It is
difficult to think of a parallel event in Christian history; the nearest
equivalent perhaps was the conquest of Constantinople in the year
1204 by the Latin Christians of the Fourth Crusade. Nor do we
know how far they enforced their beliefs upon the native population.
What is certain is that they also established a foundation in Cairo
in the form of a clearly marked out city north of the foundation of
Ibn-Tulun. It is also certain that within its boundaries they founded
what has since remained Egypt's most famous and influential
institution, the mosque of El-Azhar, which they shortly afterwards
developed into a university with the object presumably of spreading
the Shia doctrines.

The Fatimids lasted in Egypt for two hundred years but they
were two centuries which included much anarchy compounded of
assassinations, revolutions and civil and foreign wars. By contrast
the country was prospering. These were the centuries in which
the Mediterranean countries developed from small beginnings
into great commercial powers; Amalfi and Pisa, Genoa and Venice
became famous in Italy; and in the southern Mediterranean Egypt
became in some degree their counterpart. Primarily this was on
account of the Eastern trade. The route from Alexandria to Suez
was the highway of commerce and Cairo became the great commercial centre. This is the explanation of the paradox that under the
chaotic conditions of the Fatimids and their Mameluke successors
Cairo developed architecturally into the world's most splendid
city.

Among the first Caliphs of the Fatimids was Al-Hakim sometimes
labelled as the Caligula of Egypt. Al-Hakim was responsible for
the founding of a great library in aid of Shia propaganda and we
shall become aware of him at Cairo as the builder of a considerable
mosque, now sadly ruined, within the Fatimid walls. He was more
celebrated in his lifetime for his oppressions and persecutions,
among them the destruction of the Holy Sepulchre of the Christians
at Jerusalem, an act which may be taken as the first provocation
which ultimately caused the Crusades. This act was made possible
by the fact that the Fatimids, in addition to Egypt, had made
themselves masters also of Palestine and Syria; and the consequence
was that when the Crusades developed in the twelfth century Egypt

found itself in the front line. Nor were the expeditions of the Crusaders dictated solely by religion; the increasing prosperity of Egypt had made it a tempting target for invasion and plunder and during the final period of the Fatimids and in the subsequent century a number of Christian expeditions invaded both by land and sea. Most famous of these episodes was the crusade of Saint Louis (King Louis IX) of France who in 1249 landed near Damietta and advanced to Mansurah but the venture ended unhappily with the defeat and capture of the King and his army. Another new element was introduced into Egyptian history during these centuries by the Turks, a Moslem people of Central Asia who, appearing first as mercenaries, began to play an increasingly decisive role in the turbulent affairs of the Caliphs.

The most prominent figure in Egypt during the twelfth century was Saladin the famous antagonist of Richard Coeur de Lion in the Crusades. By origin a Kurd of Armenia, he was brought up at the Court of Damascus and early proved himself as a brilliant general of the Syrian ruler Nur-ed-Din. It was essential for Nur-ed-Din that Egypt should be added to his domain and this Saladin achieved. The last Fatimid ruler was deposed, Moslem orthodoxy was restored and on the death of Nur-ed-din Saladin became ruler of the country. Not much of his life was spent in Egypt for he was occupied in foreign wars, and his death occurred in Damascus where his imposing tomb survives; but his memory lives in Egypt on account of the splendid citadel which he founded and which still dominates the whole of Cairo. Though Saladin founded a dynasty, the so-called Ayyubites, his successors did him little honour; intestine feuds developéd; and one of the last of the family, desirous of increasing his military forces, took a decision which was destined to have a major and sinister effect on the later ages of Egyptian history. This was the admission and establishment of the Mamelukes or White Slaves.

The Mamelukes, as their name implied, were bought as slaves to be trained up as soldiers for the ruler and to act as his bodyguard. The first Mamelukes were probably Turks; the custom once started continued through the centuries and in the later ages the favourite country of origin was the Caucasus. The result of the introduction of such an alien body with no roots in the country and no responsibility except to a weak ruler was predictable; within a few years the ruler had been deposed and a Mameluke was seated on the throne. (The murder of this last ruler took place at Mansura under the eyes of Saint Louis of France who had been taken prisoner and incarcerated there during his unfortunate Sixth Crusade). The type of government to which Egypt was now subjected is illustrated by the fact that during the first Mameluke period (the so-called Bahri Mamelukes) twenty-five sultans ruled in 132 years. Not that some of the Mameluke sultans were not rulers of great ability. Beibars, one of the earliest rulers successfully liquidated the Crusader relics of the Kingdom of Jerusalem and carried off to Cairo an Abassid caliph to serve as nominal head of the Moslem world. The last holding of the Christians in Palestine, the fortress of Acre, was captured by another Mameluke sultan in 1291 AD.

It was during these turbulent years that Cairo, notwithstanding earthquakes, plagues and civil strife, acquired many of the buildings which have made it the outstanding architectural survival of the Middle Ages. Kalaoun, who ruled during the later thirteenth century built within the walls of the Fatimid city the outstanding group of buildings which we shall visit in Cairo and which still bear his name. Close to them is the surviving minaret of the mosque of Nasir, an early fourteenth-century ruler whose brutality of character was only equalled by his excellence in building; a more complete sample of his work is his mosque in the Cairo citadel. But the ruler who achieved the greatest architectural fame was certainly Hasan whose famous mosque has survived virtually intact.

The later Mamelukes (called Circassian) continued the architectural tradition with a series of buildings which if less imposing than their predecessors are certainly among the most decorative in Cairo. Prominent among them were Barkuk and Kait Bey whose tombs provide so magnificent a skyline in Cairo's City of the Dead. And one of the last of them was El-Ghuri whose collection of buildings at the southern end of the Fatimid city provides one of the most picturesque townscapes in Cairo. But these Mameluke sultans were not exclusively devoted to building or even to civil strife. Judged by the barbarities which they inflicted on their subjects their rule was probably among the most terrible that Egyptians have ever had to bear. But for one achievement posterity at least owes them gratitude; they kept the Mongols at bay. Unlike Syria and all the Middle Eastern countries which suffered the terrible Mongol invasion Egypt was saved and her architectural and artistic treasures were preserved.

The Mongol invasion, for all its ferocity, proved a flash in the pan. A much more permament menace were now the Turks who, from being mercenaries or slaves had organised themselves under the dynasty of Othman into an all-conquering military empire. In 1517 AD Cairo was taken by storm; the last Mameluke ruler was crucified beneath the city gate; and by a series of dubious transactions the Caliphate was transferred to the ruler of the Turks. This was the Sultan Selim I.

It was the fate of Egypt to become now once more a mere province of a great empire ruled from far away. For another half century the Turkish Empire continued to expand; then came a long and slow decline. But such was the staying power of the Turks that they remained the nominal rulers of Egypt for four centuries in all. Part of the reason for their rule becoming nominal was that though they liquidated the Mameluke rulers they did not abolish the Mamelukes themselves. A Turkish governor was always at the seat of power but as his power declined, the effective rule of Egypt began increasingly to resemble the pre-Turkish period. The dominant interest of the government in Constantinople was the annual tribute and increasingly the effective power went to the Mameluke who proved most capable of exacting it. The Turkish genius for impoverishing their conquered provinces was never better exemplified than in Egypt. Admittedly the prosperity of the country received a serious blow from a cause for which the Turks could not be blamed — the discovery of the new routes to the Far East round the Cape of Africa. But year by year the cities and the population declined and by the end of the eighteenth century it is fair to say that the government and condition of Egypt must have achieved an all-time record in oppression and in wretchedness.

It was during the Turkish period that the Western Europeans began once again to take an interest in Egypt. The Levant Company was founded in 1581; a French consul was established in Cairo; a small community of French and English merchants led a furtive life in the country and the consequence was that a small trading relationship was established. More surprisingly, a few enterprising individuals visited the country as tourists; the poet George Sandys in the early seventeenth century climbed the Great Pyramid; the ubiquitous Richard Pococke in the eighteenth century explored the Nile Valley; and for a few privileged characters Egypt beckoned as a possible extension of the Grand Tour. Meanwhile the European Powers were beginning to lengthen their political sights; if Poland was being partitioned, why should not the decaying Turkish Empire undergo the same fate? The magic of the word 'colony' began to be felt. The French government under Louis XV and Louis XVI, grievously conscious of the loss of India to the British, took an increasing interest; under their auspices the Baron de Tott arrived in 1775 with the secret mission of making a full report on the country. To all this activity the Egyptians and their swiftly changing rulers remained blandly indifferent and the traditional life continued: the field-labour of millions of peasants, the violent bickerings of the Mamelukes, the annual tribute to the Sultan. Things were in this accustomed state when one day in June 1798 the rulers in Cairo received from the governor in Alexandria the news of the arrival of a fleet: 'The fleet which has just appeared is immense. One can see neither its beginning nor its end. For the love of God and his prophet send us fighting men.' Egypt had reached a milestone in history; Western Europe in the person of Napoleon Bonaparte and his armada had arrived.

The story of this astonishing expedition has been often told and it would be futile to repeat it here. But a few verdicts may be essayed. The expedition was very large, involving hundreds of ships including warships, and tens of thousands of men. No expedition can have failed more completely in all its political and military aims. No expedition ever produced more astonishing side-effects. Bonaparte's warships were mostly sunk by Nelson in the so-called Battle of the Nile near Aboukir. Thousands of his soldiers died from disease or in battle and those who survived were eventually shipped home like cattle to the country whence they came. Bonaparte won battles; the so-called Battle of the Pyramids where his artillery destroyed the Mameluke cavalry; the second Battle of Aboukir where he drove a Turkish expeditionary force into the sea. He also suffered a disastrous defeat on an expedition into Syria. He himself deserted his army and returned to France to establish himself as First Consul. Egypt probably had never been of genuine interest to him; the expedition he viewed as a stepping-stone to higher things. The country when his forces finally left it was in much the same condition as when he had arrived.

The first spectacular side-effect was due to Bonaparte's imaginative inspiration in organising the campaign; he included in his forces a large party of French savants with some famous names like Monge and Denon. The sufferings endured by these characters through the hardships of the campaign hardly bear thinking of; undaunted by the appalling conditions, they set themselves with the indefatigible pedantry of the French savant to record and catalogue an entire country. The Pyramids and the monuments round Cairo were obvious subjects after the French domination had been assured;

it was a different matter in Upper Egypt where the only opportunity of visiting the great monuments was by attaching themselves as supernumeraries when characters like General Desaix were sent on punitive expeditions to chastise evasive Mamelukes. Incredibly, the task to which they set themselves was done. Shipped back to France with the rest of the expedition they got down to work; in 1802 Denon produced his great book on the expedition of General Napoleon Bonaparte and in 1809 appeared the first of many gigantic volumes of plates published by the order of Napoleon the Great. Thus were laid the great foundations of that study which has so greatly prospered in subsequent years, the study of Egyptology.

The other remarkable side-effect of Bonaparte's expedition was the emergence of Mehemet Ali. Mehemet Ali was an Albanian Turk who had taken service with the Sultan and was among those Turkish soldiers who at the second battle of Aboukir were driven into the sea. Managing to save himself he continued his military career and contrived to rise rapidly to an important post of command; so well was he thought of by the Turkish sultan that he was appointed Viceroy. In 1807 he successfully defeated an attempted British invasion. Four years later he achieved a fundamental reform; inviting all the chief Mamelukes to a gathering at the Citadel in Cairo, he ambushed them and succeeded in massacring the whole tribe. From then on, under the nominal suzerainty of the Sultan, he was the effective master of Egypt and founded a dynasty that was destined to survive until the year 1952.

Mehemet Ali was a crude and unlettered savage of the most tyrannical type but he proved himself a most effective ruler. Both European and Asiatic powers were made aware that Egypt had become once again a formidable military power. Under his capable son Ibrahim Pasha successful expeditions were mounted in Arabia and the Sudan; Egyptian armies intervened in the Greek War of Independence; Syria and Palestine were conquered; and at one moment, after he had fallen out with his suzerain, Mehemet Ali even threatened the survival of the Turkish Empire. More important for his subjects were his internal reforms. A sensible administration was imposed, health measures initiated, education introduced. The first great steps were taken towards the improvement of agriculture by the construction of the Delta Barrage and innumerable irrigation canals; the country was dotted with factories for making textiles and refining sugar; above all, Mehemet Ali provided Egypt with his greatest gift, the introduction of cotton. Ever since, cotton has been the gold of Egypt.

Mehemet Ali was unlucky in his family; his son Ibrahim pre-deceased him; the succession went to Abbas, Said and Ismail. Under Said was continued the policy consistently followed by Mehemet Ali of developing the country with the aid of the finance and expertise of France. With the aid of a remarkable Frenchman Ferdinand de Lesseps he launched Egypt on its most remarkable nineteenth-century venture, the Suez Canal. After fifteen years of appalling vicissitudes the Canal was triumphantly opened by Ismail in 1869 in the presence of the French Empress Eugénie and the assembled heads of the European powers. Meanwhile Ismail, who had acquired the title Khedive, by his extravagance was rapidly ruining the country. In 1875 he was reduced to the necessity of selling his interest in the Canal to the British Government and in the following year he faced national bankruptcy. His indignant European creditors demanded action; a Franco-British con-dominium of control was imposed; in 1879 Ismail was made to abdicate in favour of his son Tewfik; and four years later Great Britain assumed full responsibility for the administration of the country under its Consul-General Sir Evelyn Baring, subsequently Lord Cromer.

The reigns of Mehemet Ali and his successors were the great age of Egyptian exploration. The publication of the great French volumes on the country aroused passionate interest in the West; in the post-Napoleonic generation the Egyptian mode became the rage in decoration, furniture, buildings; Piccadilly had its 'Egyptian Hall' and in Dublin even a railway station was built to look like the pylon of an ancient Egyptian temple. To those who sought to discover and acquire the artistic treasures of the country the Mehemet Ali dynasty offered unique opportunities; as Moslem rulers they had no interest in securing or preserving the relics of the religion of previous ages; as dedicated Westerners they were keen to introduce European finance and enterprise into every aspect of Egyptian life. The appetite of the cognoscenti had already been whetted by the discovery during Bonaparte's expedition of the Rosetta Stone (now in the British Museum) which provided the clue to ancient hieroglyphics. With the restoration of order and settled administration by Mehemet Ali the cultural invaders descended on the country. In the first decades it was a competition between the French and the English. Soon Egypt was being stripped of thousands of portable antiquities by a steady stream of collectors, dealers, tourists and shady dealers who saw a chance of a quick profit from the antiquities trade. Among the remarkable characters

of this period was the circus strong man Belzoni who after displaying
his muscular strength in London and elsewhere decided to make
a career in Egyptology. Arriving in Cairo he allied himself with
the British Consul General, Salt; among his first exploits was an
expedition to Upper Egypt to secure, in the face of intense French
competition, the huge granite head of Rameses II which is now to
be seen in the British Museum under the name of the Young
Memnon. The Valley of the Kings at Thebes became one of his
major targets; he made important discoveries in the Giza pyramids
themselves. Meanwhile the French and their agents were equally
busy. A steady stream of Egyptian objects, large and small, flowed
to the countries of Western Europe. The two major destinations
were the British Museum and the Louvre but the unlikeliest places
were included; the alabaster tomb of the Pharaoh Seti I went to
the London house of the architect Sir John Soane and a large
obelisk from Philae landed up in the garden of Kingston Lacy
House in Dorset on a site chosen by the Duke of Wellington.

For the development of a more responsible attitude to Egyptian
antiquities the chief credit must go to the French. Without ever
having been to Egypt the young savant Champollion, after years
of study at last broke the secret of the hieroglyphics and when he
at length visited the country it became possible for the first time
to read and understand the inscriptions of the Ancient Egyptians.
Appalled by the looting and destruction which at that time was
universal, Champollion made a personal appeal to Mehemet Ali;
the consequence was a decree forbidding the export of antiquities,
appointing an Inspector and authorising the construction of a
museum in Egypt itself. This was the first step in a long, long
battle, in which the chief antagonists were the indifference and
inactivity of the Egyptian rulers and the greed and intense activity
of the dealers and tomb robbers.

The great British pioneer of Egyptology was Sir Gardner
Wilkinson, who without any Government support surveyed ancient
sites, translated inscriptions and hieroglyphics and wrote the first
great work on the Ancient Egyptians. The French tradition was
continued by Mariette, who from the humblest beginnings worked
his way into the Louvre, mastered everything about Egyptology
and finally got himself sent to Egypt. The country became his
lifework; he surveyed, excavated and translated with tireless energy
and was eventually rewarded by being appointed director of the
non-existent Egyptian museum which eventually took shape at
Bulak, the river-port of Cairo. Mariette's death at the end of the

1870s coincided with the bankruptcy of Ismail and the arrival of Sir Evelyn Baring on the Egyptian scene.

Though the French had surrendered political control to the British, they were anxious not to lose their leading position in Egyptian archaeology, and they were able to arrange to have another Frenchman, Maspero appointed as Mariette's successor. His appointment coincided with some sensational discoveries by tomb robbers in the Valley of the Kings and an enormous resulting commerce in mummies, statues and objects of every kind. With the co-operation of Baring, Maspero was able to build up an Inspectorate of Antiquities and recover some control, but the museums of the world were now for practical purposes in league with the robbers and even the British Museum had its buying agent. An important British initiative in the 1880s was the Egypt Exploration Fund. It was the directors of this fund who discovered Flinders Petrie and it was Flinders Petrie who imported a new standard of responsibility and care into surveying and excavation and established Egyptology in its modern form. Important pioneering work was done in the Delta and the Faiyum but even now the end result could be disappointing; a splendid collection of mummy-portraits which Petrie despatched to Bulak was dumped outside the museum to rot in the spring rains. Then he switched to the immensely important site of Amarna where he employed among others a young man called Howard Carter destined to be the most sensational name in Egyptology. And later to Abydos.

In the later nineteenth century Egypt ceased to be the exclusive prerogative of the English and the French. As early as 1842 the King of Prussia had become interested and sent an expedition under Lepsius. In later years Germans, Italians and Americans all made major contributions. And yet the biggest success went to the British. The young Howard Carter, after half a lifetime of excavation in the Valley of the Kings, achieved at length in 1922 under the auspices of Lord Carnarvon his ultimate triumph, the discovery of the intact tomb of the Pharaoh Tutankhamen.

From this archaeological summary it might be thought that Ancient Egypt was the major pre-occupation of the newly imposed British regime. In fact its chief concern was a sustained effort to bring Egypt into the modern world. The regime instituted by Sir Evelyn Baring was of that type in which the later British Empire specialised, a strange compound of dedication and self-interest, in which a genuine desire to improve the condition of the ruled was fused with a sense of British Imperial interests. Egypt in this scheme

of things had its special eccentricities: the Turkish Sultan continued
as Suzerain; the Egyptian Khedive continued as ruler; the Egyptian
government departments continued as administrators; only in every
part of the administration were introduced British officials as
advisers, executants or consultants on Egyptian policy. For the
population the result was good; the appalling tyrannies of the
Egyptian rulers were gradually eased; torture was abolished; taxes
were made regular; health services were developed; the power of
the money-lender was curtailed. Great new steps were taken in
the realm of agriculture; the first great barrage was built at Assuan;
and much was done to develop Mehemet Ali's cotton industry. By
the time of the First World War Egypt was reckoned to be in effect
a British possession; Turkish sovereignty was finally disclaimed;
and a state of war between Turks and Britons rapidly developed
along the Suez Canal. Egypt was spared the horrors of war and the
price of cotton rose to unheard of heights.

A side-effect of the Baring regime was the development of the
tourist trade. Already in the time of Ismail one could go by steamer
from Brindisi to Alexandria, by train from Alexandria to Cairo
and by small steamer from Cairo to Luxor and Assuan. Few tourists
can have done foreign travel more luxuriously than the future
King Edward VII when he made the Nile trip as Ismail's guest in
1869; he was provided with a flotilla of six blue and gold steamers
each towing a barge carrying among other things four riding horses,
a milk white donkey for Princess Alexandra, 3000 bottles of cham-
pagne and 4000 of claret, four French chefs and a laundry. From
England, always remarkable for its female eccentrics, there had
come about the same time Amelia Edwards, authoress of *A Thousand
Miles up the Nile* which, published in 1877, became Egypt's most
popular travel-book; and Lucie Duff-Gordon, who actually established herself for some years in a house built on the roof of the
Temple of Luxor. The opening of the Suez Canal, a convenient
half-way house on the journey to India, enormously increased the
traffic. Shepheards was already established as the visitor's favourite
rendezvous in Cairo, the famous Mena House came into being
beside the Pyramids and soon luxurious winter hotels were being
built at Luxor and Assuan. This was the great age of the dragoman,
the enterprising native anxious to take the private tourist under
his wing. And for the more expensive tourist it was the great age
of the dahabeah, the private sailing-boat with its private crew able
to do the whole journey up the Nile and back.

Much of this way of life, like many other good things, came to an end with the First World War. But much of the social life survived. It was not one in which the Egyptians themselves played much part. In Alexandria it was the local international set—French, Greeks, Italians—who set the pace and vied with each other in the elaboration and luxury of their entertainments. In Cairo the tone was decidedly English. The famous Gezira Club with its great racecourse was a notable centre of fashion. Nothing was pleasanter than to dance all night and as dawn came up ride out to Mena House for an early morning swim followed by a large breakfast before going out in the desert to shoot; and after a siesta spend the afternoon at the Club in preparation for dressing for dinner and starting the whole thing over again. All this did not greatly benefit Egypt; the organisation was generally in the hands of Swiss or Germans or Italians and it was they who profited.

But some of these things now began to be noticed. Egypt, shortly to become an independent kingdom but still largely under British control, became a more matter-of-fact country increasingly adapting itself to a twentieth-century role. And in the twentieth century, for the first time for many centuries, the voice of the Egyptian people began to make itself heard. Admittedly it was the voice primarily of that small proportion of the nation which thanks to the improvement in conditions had acquired education, sometimes some property and the capacity for independent ideas. Nothing in human existence is less appreciated than good administration and when this is imposed by foreigners it can be made to look an intolerable offence. The dawning political consciousness of the Egyptian people inevitably acquired an anti-British tone. The austere Cromer was followed in the twentieth century by the informal Gorst and the portentous Kitchener. Parliamentary government with an Egyptian Prime Minister was instituted, a Nationalist Party came into being and Egypt acquired its first political hero, Suad Zagloul. So long as the First World War lasted Zagloul kept the ardour of the Nationalists in check. But with the inauguration of the Peace Conference in 1919 came the demand that Egypt, like many other countries, should have political independence. The period between the two world wars was one of agitation, negotiation, compromise, pock-marked with outbursts of revolt and violence. In 1922 independence was proclaimed and the then Khedive Fuad became a King, but in reality much British control remained. The elections were now won by the party called the Wafd and a curious triangle of power developed between the Wafd, the Egyptian monarch and the British High Commissioner. By a Treaty made in 1936 British troops were withdrawn to the Canal Zone and apart from some specific reservations total power was handed over to the Egyptian parties. Simultaneously King Fuad died, to be succeeded by his son Farouk.

Progress was soon halted by the threat of the Second World War. Egypt became once more a key point in the strategy of Britain and her allies and the country increasingly acquired the appearance of an armed camp. Egyptian public opinion was embarrassingly divided, the fear of Hitler and Mussolini balanced by the urge to be finally rid of the British. The position became critical in 1942 when Germans and Italians advanced to within a hundred miles of Alexandria; Mussolini was said to have had a white horse shipped over for his state entry and for some months the country faced the prospect of being incorporated in an Italian Empire covering the whole of the North-eastern area of the African continent and stretching from the Western Mediterranean to the Indian Ocean. Farouk himself wavered; British tanks and armoured cars invaded the Abdin Palace; and a pro-British government had to be forcibly installed. The emergency was brought to an end by Montgomery's victory at Alamein. With the restoration of peace the political battle was joined once more.

But now increasingly there were elements in public opinion that saw little that was good either in the British or in their own political leaders or in their own Egyptian monarch. The post-war years were the years of the crimes, the follies and the excesses of King Farouk. While Farouk squandered and womanised, revolutionary groups particularly in the army plotted and recruited. Nothing was said in public and little was known; among the most active and successful of the plotters was Captain Gamal Abdel Nasser, the leader of the so-called Free Officers. Things were in this state when in 1948 the British evacuated Palestine and Egypt was suddenly confronted with the State of Israel. Inadequately armed and incompetently commanded, the Egyptian army was launched into war with the Israelis and suffered humiliating defeat. Disillusion was now total; among the Free Officers the last shreds of faith in the *ancien régime* disappeared. Guerilla war was now launched with the connivance of the Egyptian auxiliary police on the British forces still in the Canal Zone; early in 1952 the British Commander reacted by surrounding a police headquarters and gunning down its occupants; and the balloon went up.

Who was responsible for what then happened in Cairo is not very certain. From an early hour the mobs were on the streets. A fight broke out in a cabaret near the Opera; within minutes the building was in flames. In other parts of the city men with paraffin and blazing torches were methodically setting fire to buildings that were known to be foreign-owned. A lorry load of men drove up to Shepheards hotel, sprayed the rooms with inflammable powder and set the whole building ablaze. The government sat back and did nothing; the King was busy entertaining 400 officers to lunch; by the evening 400 buildings in the city centre had been burnt down or destroyed.

This outburst was the prelude to political revolution. From now on, between the Free Officers and the regime, it was a secret war to the death. In July the Officers decided they were ready; a figurehead was found in General Neguib; the army headquarters was captured, then the broadcasting station and the airport; in a surprisingly short time Cairo was in the insurgents' hands. Farouk and the Prime Minister were at Alexandria; an attempted counter coup came to nothing; the King was faced with an ultimatum, exile or death. With 204 pices of luggage he embarked on the royal yacht and vanished from history; it was the end of a dynasty and the end of an era.

From the start of the new regime the real ruler was Nasser and his principal lieutenant was Anwar-el-Sadat. The reality was made apparent in 1954 when Neguib was set aside and something like a police state was imposed. The new rulers knew what they wanted to get rid of; it was not so clear what they wanted to create. The first target was still the British and in 1954 Nasser secured an agreement by which their soldiers went. Nasser became overnight a hero of the Arab world. The Israelis took advantage of the resulting power-vacuum to launch a sudden attack at Gaza and the question of military rearmament became the first priority. The issue was a fateful one; it meant that Egypt henceforward was caught up in the developing confrontation between East and West.

In the early stages of the new regime the Americans had been friendly. They had given moral support over the Canal Zone treaty; they dropped encouraging hints about finance for the gigantic project upon which the Nasser regime was now resolved, the new Assuan High Dam. But then, despite American pressure, Nasser refused to join the American-sponsored Middle East alliance. The Americans retaliated by refusing to sell arms. What followed was two years of fast footwork. The Russians came up with an offer of arms sales. Nasser discovered that the Israelis were being armed by the French; he himself signed up with the Russians. Then he turned again to the West; an agreement was made that the World Bank, supported by America and Britain, would finance the Assuan Dam. While the Israelis were armed by the French, Nasser gave secret support to the Arabs fighting a war to the death against the French in Algeria. The support of the World Bank for the Assuan Dam was confirmed. Then a thunderbolt descended; the Americans followed shortly by the British withdrew their support from the project.

For Nasser and his prestige the blow was shattering and a swift public political reaction was required. At a hasty consultation, the decision was taken, and later publicly announced by Nasser to an excited crowd in Alexandria: the Suez Canal Company would be nationalised. For Britain and France, the countries most interested, this was a public insult and a large-scale injury; combined with what was happening in Algeria, it looked as if the Western European Powers would be completely eliminated from North Africa. Troop movements began.

As if the situation was not already sufficiently complicated, two new factors intervened. First, the Americans took alarm and began to try to damp down the situation which they primarily had provoked. Secondly, the Israelis, angered by further Egyptian provocations, began to plan a limited war. The stage was set for the brief but vivid episode known as Suez.

Thanks to American insistence and the influence of the United Nations the effective military operations were limited to a few days. The Israelis invaded Sinai, the British and French invaded the Canal Zone and Port Said was largely destroyed by bombardment. But the end-product of all this was success for Nasser; the invading forces were withdrawn and the Suez Canal Company remained nationalised. What was of major importance for the future of Egypt was that a mass expulsion of foreigners was initiated, not limited to the English and the French. It was a major step towards making Egypt a truly Arab-controlled country. It was followed in 1961 with a major assault on the wealthy Egyptian bourgeoisie itself; huge confiscations and nationalisations occurred and the Greeks who had so far escaped were involved also in the catastrophe. Egypt had almost become a totalitarian national State. It also became for the first time in centuries more puritanical; it was decreed that the belly-dancers had to cover up their navels. More remarkably, tarbouches (relics of Turkish tyranny) ceased to be worn.

Nasser's positive initiatives flowed principally in three directions. First, in the rehabilitation and development of the country. Building on the foundations of the British administration, he enormously developed schools, medical services, water supplies, road construction, house building. Important attempts were made to establish new industries, notably the great steel works at Helouan. The second initiative was in inter-Arab politics. This initiative, irresistible apparently to Arab rulers, brought virtually no profit to Egypt. A union was made with Syria, and subsequently abandoned, under the title of United Arab Republic. Intrigues were fomented in Iraq and Lebanon and Jordan; plots were constantly made against Israel. The third initiative was in the development of relations with the Eastern bloc, notably Russia.

This was the serious long-term consequence of the Suez episode. The Russians, sensing their opportunity, moved in and said that they would finance and build the Assuan Dam. Instead of the French and British soldiers thousands of Russian engineers and technicians descended on the soil of Egypt. Kruschev himself came to the inaugural ceremony and there created Nasser a Hero of the Soviet Union. And the Russians brought also much-needed arms. The stage was being set for another military episode, for Egypt was still linked with Syria and Syrian-Israeli relations were reaching an all-time low. Nasser himself raised the stakes in 1965 by deliberately blocking Israeli shipping in the Red Sea. The result was predictable; Israel attacked.

The resulting war was another disaster for Egypt. The much vaunted jet aeroplanes from Russia were bombed and pulverised on their airfields. The Egyptian Army in Sinai was annihilated. It was the Six Day War. For Nasser it was a political and a personal disaster; there was nothing left for him but to resign and disappear. He came to the microphone and announced his decision to the Egyptian people. And then an astonishing thing happened, a massive national reaction: Nasser was still their hero, he must not go. And he was persuaded to stay on. He ruled for another five years until his sudden death in 1970, when he was given a funeral as for a national hero. When one thinks what he had done to Egypt, this is extraordinary; apart from appalling losses in materials and men, he had left the Suez Canal blocked and useless, Egypt's oil fields in Israeli hands and the cotton crop mortgaged for years ahead to the Russians. The explanation must be that for the first time for centuries he had given the Egyptian people a government that they could feel was their own.

He was succeeded, as he would have wished, by his second-in-command Anwar-el-Sadat. It must have been a daunting inheritance.

1 Pompey's Pillar, Alexandria

2 Cairo: Looking over the city from the minaret of the Mosque of Ibn
  Tulun. On the left are the Mosques of Er Rifa'i and Sultan Hasan. To
  the right is the citadel and the mosque of Mehemet Ali

3 Cairo: A close-up of the mosque of Ibn Tulun

4   Cairo: The mosque of Sultan Hasan

5   Cairo: A street scene in the Fatimid City with the old Fatimid Gate, the Bab Zoueila, in
    the background. On top of the Gate are the two minarets of the mosque of Al Muayyad

6   Cairo: The tomb-mosque of Kuait Bey in the City of the Dead

7 Beneath the date palms – a village near Karnak
8 Giza: The Sphinx with the Great Pyramid on the left

9 The Meidum Pyramid

10   Abydos: The Hypostyle Hall of the Temple of Seti

11   Dendera: the Birth House of Horus

12 Karnak: Obelisk of Queen Hatshepsut, Temple of Amun

13 Karnak: Rameses II and his wife, Temple of Amun

14 Tomb of Queen Hatshepsut, Deir el Bahari, Thebes

15 Edfu: statue of Horus the hawk god. On the wall an offering is made to
Horus who wears the double crown of Upper and Lower Egypt

16 Kom Ombo Temple on the banks of the Nile

17 Donkeys are the transport for passengers at Beni Hasan

18 Upper Egypt: The Colossi of Memnon at Thebes

19 Feluccas awaiting visitors, Assuan

5　THE DELTA AND LOWER EGYPT

The Delta is that triangle of Egypt whose points are at Alexandria, Port Said and Cairo. A more singular stretch of the earth's surface it would be hard to find; the whole area has been raised from out of the Mediterranean sea-bed by the thousands of years of deposit of the Nile silt. Before the era of the great dams the Nile in its months of inundation over-ran great stretches of the countryside; Herodotus in his description of his tour claims that he travelled over most of the Delta by boat. Human life was carried on in the villages raised a few feet above the flood level until the waters subsided and agriculture could be resumed.

The Nile in ancient times had numerous branches. These are now contracted to two, emerging respectively at Rosetta and Damietta. The annual floods resulted in the curious lakes which fringe the sea-board; Mariout, which we have already seen at Alexandria; Edkon, Borollos and Manzaleh. Their effect is to render difficult communications along the Mediterranean coast. Rosetta can be visited from Alexandria, Damietta from Port Said; they contain nothing for the student of Ancient Egypt but are not without appeal to the romantic lover of Islamic architecture. Rosetta during the eclipse of Alexandria became Egypt's principal port and a place of some significance; Damietta was sufficiently well known to be chosen as the target for St Louis' unfortunate crusade. Both places provide the opportunity of savouring traditional Islam without the attendant pandemonium of modern Cairo. Rosetta in particular preserves great character from the manner of its street architecture, sequences of great brick houses corbelled outwards so as almost to meet overhead and copiously provided with those wooden grills which give so unfair an advantage to the observer from within as compared with the observer from without.

Uniquely in modern Egypt this is a city whose population, since the re-emergence of Alexandria, has been in decline. Damietta, with some 100,000 inhabitants, is more of this world. But it too has its romantic streets, and two of its mosques, the El-Bahr and the El-Gabanch, are worth a glance. In Rosetta the mosques are dated to a century unfamiliar in Egyptian building, the seventeenth century AD. The largest is the much-columned mosque of Zagloul; then there is the mosque of Mahamet-Thuleti remarkable for its ornamentation in local tiles; and finally the picturesque ensemble of the mosque of Mahomet-el-Abbasi. And Rosetta retains ramparts with an imposing exterior view.

Very different from Rosetta are most of the other towns and cities of the Delta. For this area is the power house of Egypt and the towns and cities are its evidence. These closely packed agglomerations, continually expanding their limits under the population pressures of the twentieth century, are the centres in which the hard labour of the Delta population is turned to production and profit. There can be few areas of the world where the labour is more intense. The railways from Alexandria to Cairo, or from Ismailia to Cairo, with their accompanying roads, provide an astonishing moving panorama of this essentially agricultural scene. Hundreds, if not thousands of villages pockmark the landscape, varied at intervals by a town; but the towns and villages are not more remarkable than the fields and holdings, intensively cultivated and often themselves populated to excess by the field workers. Though the Mediterranean zone has always enjoyed a winter rainfall, the whole economy now as ever is dependent on flowing water. With the modern control of the Nile and the disappearance of the inundations, irrigation has become of even more vital importance and nothing is more impressive than the intricate network of canals, irrigation channels, roads, paths and branch railways by which the whole economy of the area is sustained.

It would seem inconceivable that in this spreading ant-hill there is anything to interest or detain the visitor; and taking the word visitor at its usual modern meaning, this is sadly true. But the area has provided a fund of interest for the special visitor, namely the archaeologist; and a number of them with the dedication and endurance of their race have in the last hundred and fifty years laboured to retrace the Delta's forgotten history. For the ordinary visitor, intent upon the Pyramids or the great temples of Upper Egypt, it is inconceivable that the Delta ever offered comparisons in such fields. Yet the verdict of archaeology appears to be that through the ups and downs of the millennia and dynasties of Egypt the part played by the Delta was at least as important as the more famous upper valley of the Nile. Tanis and Bubastis in the eastern Delta were successively the capitals of the Pharaohs of the Twenty-first and Twenty-second Dynasties, and important Greek cities were established under the later Pharaohs, for example at Naucratis. Sais, a few miles north-west of the modern Tanta, had been another capital and was still a place of importance in the time of Herodotus who stayed there long enough to be told several tall stories by one of its high priests.

The excavation of these and other sites has been a labour of love, a labour also of hardship and endurance. It has been a work not without profit for there has been a considerable yield of objects and trophies to enrich still further the Egyptian museums of the world. And it has added, in terms of records, some astonishing items to the list of the creations of Ancient Egypt. The cat cemetery of Bubastis is a case in point; this was an area of several acres from which countless mummified cats have been excavated together with numerous bronze statuettes of cats. And the temple of Tanis must have been one of the greatest of all Egyptian buildings. A thousand feet in length, it was enclosed in a wall of 3,500 feet, said to be 80 feet thick and 45 feet high and to have contained twenty million bricks. But it is necessary that ordinary appetites should not be whetted by such descriptions. As one enthusiastic antiquary sadly confesses: 'Tanis is left devoid of many of its most interesting features...the ruins of the great temple are in a state of indescribable confusion...the plums have been extracted from the pudding.' Equally sad is the confession about the cats: 'Unless to one who has a passion for the historic area on which cats were emblems of divinity, the ruins...do not offer any attraction which is sufficient to repay even the slight trouble of a visit.'

Man is the greatest destroyer of the works of man; the destruction is greatest where population is greatest; and it is probably true that through many ages the Egyptian Delta has been one of the most thickly populated areas in the world. A Pharaoh dies, a dynasty decays, a priesthood evaporates; the great temples and palaces which they founded lose their purpose and their use; one generation and they become a stone quarry, an invaluable resource for the building activities of the indefatigable fellaheen. This, rather than sieges or earthquakes, must explain what is from the tourist's point of view the vacuity of the Delta. As the eye becomes more perceptive, one can see in the Delta scenery other landmarks than towns and villages. These are the great brown heaps or excrescences which so often interrupt the level plain. These surely are the sites of the urban centres of former ages, despoiled above ground of any objects of use or value and contributing little or nothing to the beauty of the Delta scene.

A similar vacuity has confronted those eager seekers who have attempted to identify the Biblical sites of Egypt. The Old Testament narrative states very specifically that the Israelites dwelt in the Land of Goschen and that under the oppression of their taskmasters they built for Pharaoh treasure cities at Pithon and Raamses. The Land of Goschen has been generally supposed to be that part of the eastern Delta which lies to the west of Ismailia. Pithon was thought to have been discovered and identified in the eighties of the last century, but the usual arguments of archaeologists have supervened and the sites of both Pithon and Raamses remain still in doubt. There is somewhat more agreement about the city of Taphanhes which figures in *Jeremiah* and which is though to be represented by the mound of Tell Defenneh some six miles west of the Suez Canal near Kantara. But in general the melancholy verdict stands good of the archaeologist, James Baikie, whom we have already quoted: 'It cannot be too plainly stated that no one has the right to say that any single scriptural statement has as yet been either proved or disproved by the results of excavation.'

But the Delta, as a glance at the map will show, is only a small triangle on the face of Lower Egypt. On each side are the enclosing deserts, vast in area as they are empty of people. The few Bedouin who do inhabit them have little in common with the fellaheen either of the Delta or the Nile Valley.

The Western or Libyan desert captured the headlines of the world in the years 1940-42 when it became the theatre of the long-drawn-out struggle between the British Eighth Army which was defending Egypt and the Italian armies from Libya who were later supported by the German Afrika Korps. After Italy had entered the Second World War in June 1940, an Italian army had occupied the border area of the Egyptian desert and remained there un-challenged until it was suddenly annihilated by a well-planned British attack in the subsequent December. This battle, generally called Sidi Barrani after the nearest place name on the coast, threw the Italians completely out of Egyptian territory and moved the theatre of war further west into Libya. But final victory was not to come so easily. By April of 1941 the Eighth Army was back on the Egyptian frontier and a fierce battle in the following month, in which the German general Rommel first made his mark, left some of the frontier posts in German-Italian hands. A further frontier battle of critical importance followed in November. But the crisis of the campaign came in June 1942 when Rommel launched an attack which penetrated three hundred miles into Egypt and was only brought to a halt at Alamein less than a hundred miles from Alexandria. It was now, as commonly asserted, that the splendid white horse was commissioned for the Italian dictator Mussolini so that he could ride in triumph into the city. Generals Alexander and Montgomery were put in charge and henceforward the campaign became personalised into a duel between Montgomery and Rommel. The turning-point came in October when Montgomery was once more able to attack. In the battle of Alamein the Germans and Italians were decisively beaten and thrown out of Egypt, never to return.

There is little now in the Western Desert to recall these epic struggles. The main German memorial is at Tobruk over the Libyan frontier. Two miles beyond the station of Alamein is a South African monument and to the left of the main coast road is the large British cemetery. Further along, on the right, is the cemetery of the Italians and the Germans. This coast road leads from Alexandria and its principal object is Mersa Matruh. This was an ancient city where Cleopatra is said to have had a palace and a naval base; it is now an agreeable town of moderate size with an impressive beach and an obvious future as a tourist resort. Beyond Mersah Matruh the landmarks thin out; Sidi Barrani was a name in the war communiqués of 1940-42; and Sir Winston Churchill records being impressed by a signal from a junior officer announcing that he had reached the second B in Bugbug. The last Egyptian post, some three hundred miles from Alexandria, is Sollum which faces the Libyan frontier station of Fort Capuzzo.

Southwards from the coast road the desert stretches, inhospitable and limitless to the southern Egyptian frontier and far beyond in the Soudan. A remarkable geographical feature, only some fifty miles south of Mersah Matruh, is the Katara Depression, an extensive desert zone which at its base is some four hundred feet below the level of the Mediterranean. The principal human feature of the West Desert is the Oasis of Siwa, some two hundred miles south of Mersah Matruh, which became famous in ancient times on account of the visit paid by Alexander the Great. Here dwelt the oracle of Zeus Ammon and here it was that the young conqueror was formally hailed as the son of the God.

An easier excursion than Siwa is the Wadi Natroun. This is a valley in the desert containing a number of salt lakes, from which valuable salt and soda are obtained. In very early Christian times the area became a resort of monks and hermits on a large scale; a recent excavation at Kellia not far away has exposed the foundations of not less than seven hundred monasteries and hermitages. In the Wadi Natroun itself four of these monasteries have survived to the present day; they are thought to be the most ancient Christian foundations in existence. What has made them a practicable excursion for the tourist is the modern 'desert road' which now forms the quickest link between Alexandria and Cairo. From the Wadi Natroun rest house a desert track leads five or six miles westwards to the Deir-es-Sourani (Syrian Convent) and two other monasteries not far away. The prospect of these constructions seen from afar and in their desert setting is not the least romantic of Egyptian experiences. Square or rectangular and built of stone, they stand like individual fortresses in this sea of sand, monuments of antique mystery. A small entrance portal leads to a small interior courtyard. The visit is soon accomplished and curiosity is quickly satisfied; in truth, though there is much that is quaint and unfamiliar, these monasteries are not architectural masterpieces nor do they now contain great treasures, though it is recorded that in the last century some thousand volumes from the Syrian convent were removed to the British Museum. The fourth monastery (Saint Macarius) can be reached by a desert track leaving the main road some ten miles further on.

So banal a description may be contrasted with the impression made on Robert Curzon who visited these monasteries in the year 1833. Of the Souriani monastery, where in the oil cellar he had found an astonishing jumble of ancient books and manuscripts, he records the prospect from the parapet. 'I could look over the wall on the left hand upon the desert, whose dusty plains stretched out as far as I could see, in hot and dreary loneliness to the horizon.... On my right how different was the scene! There below my feet lay the convent garden in all the fresh luxuriance of tropical vegetation. Tufts upon tufts of waving palms overshadowed the immense succulent leaves of the banana, which in their turn rose out of the thickets of the pomegranate rich with its bright green leaves and its blossoms of that beautiful and vivid red which is excelled by few even of the most brilliant flowers of the East. These were contrasted with the deep dark green of the caroub or locust-tree; and the yellow apples of the lotus vied with the clusters of green limes with their sweet white flowers which luxuriated in a climate too hot and sultry for the golden fruit of the orange....'

The Eastern confines of Egypt present features and problems strikingly different from anything in the Western Desert. The first feature is the Suez Canal which marks the Eastern limit of the Delta before continuing southwards to its junction with the Red Sea.

The first feature is the Suez Canal which marks the Eastern limit of the Delta before continuing southwards to its junction with the Red Sea.

From the earliest times the Egyptian rulers had realised the peculiar situation of Lower Egypt forming a bridgehead between the great land masses of Africa and Asia and at various epochs projects had been formulated for making a water connection to the Red Sea from the Mediterranean. A canal is thought to have been effectively in operation under the Middle Kingdom from a branch of the Nile near Bubastis to Lake Timsah via the Wadi-el-Tumilat or land of Goschen; continuing thence southwards approximately along the course of the present canal. According to Herodotus a major effort was made by the Pharaoh Necho of the Twenty-sixth Dynasty to re-open this canal, in the course of which 120,000 Egyptians perished. It is certain that after the Persian conquest this canal was completed by the Emperor Darius and the canal system appears to have been extended under the early Ptolemies. Before the Roman conquest the canal seems to have fallen into disrepair and was then again put in order by the Emperor Trajan under the name of Amnis Trajanus. The Arab conquerors are also recorded as having restored it but it appears to have become permanently unserviceable after the eighth century AD. In more modern times a number of projects were put forward for restoring communication between the two seas; more than one French mission reported on it in the reigns of Louis XIV and XV, and Bonaparte actually ordered works of excavation to begin. But all in vain. The project finally came to fruition through the efforts of a remarkable nineteenth-century Frenchman Ferdinand de Lesseps. Lesseps started life as a civil servant in the consular department and among other posts was Consul for some years at Alexandria where his friendship with Said, a son of Mehemet Ali, led to an interest in a possible canal. Retiring from the consular service in the 1850s after Said had become Pasha, he worked out the details of a scheme and was given a first territorial concession. The work was formally started in 1859 and received the warm encouragement of Said's successor Ismail.

So ambitious an undertaking clearly entailed great demands in the spheres both of finance and of labour. Lesseps created the Compagnie Universelle du Canal Maritime de Suez and invited subscriptions from the whole world; in fact most of the shares were taken up by the French while a considerable residue remained in the hands of Ismail. Labour was secured by what was in effect a corvée, enforced by the Pasha; it was not very successful and in the later stages most of the work was mechanically done. The work was completed in 1869 and the opening of the canal was made a great occasion by Ismail. The Empress Eugénie of France was invited as the guest of honour, an inaugural ceremony was staged at Port Said and on the 16th November a convoy of sixty-eight vessels of various nationalities, headed by the Empress, made the first passage. Verdi was commissioned to compose an opera and produced *Aida*, but unfortunately too late for the event and *Rigoletto* had to be performed instead.

The British government, though it must clearly be concerned by a project so directly affecting the communication with India, remained for long disinterested and at times appeared hostile to the whole idea. The canal once completed, it became rapidly clear that British ships would be the principal users, and it was their patronage that rescued the Company from a condition perilously close to bankruptcy. Hence it was not unnatural that the ownership and control of the waterway should become increasingly a matter of official concern. In 1875 it was the Khedive Ismail who was approaching bankruptcy; rumours began to circulate that his holding of Suez Canal shares was on offer; Disraeli secured the services and co-operation of Rothschilds; and the upshot was that the whole of the Khedive's holding became the property of the British government. It was frequently stated and accepted in later years that the British owned the Suez Canal; in fact the British government, though substantial shareholders, were still minority shareholders; the company remained an international company managed in Paris; and the only concession made to the British was the right to nominate two or three directors to the Board. The Company over the years became exceedingly profitable.

In 1884 an international convention was signed which declared the canal to be open to vessels of all nations, whether of commerce or of war. This situation was necessarily modified in the First World War, when the British undertook the defence of Egypt and the Suez Canal became in effect a front line against the Turks. In this period originated the term 'Suez Canal Zone' which became so familiar through the next fity years. In the Second World War the Suez Canal, no longer a front line against the Turks, was a prize as valuable as Egypt itself and the successful defence of Egypt meant that it was never seriously at risk from the Axis Powers. The post-war negotiations between the Egyptian and British governments resulted in an accord whereby the British, while evacuating their troops from the country as a whole, would continue to garrison the Canal Zone. These arrangements were destined to be violently upset by the events of 1956.

These events were triggered off, as we have seen, by the American decision to withdraw from financing the new project of the Assuan dam. Nasser's reaction was to decree the nationalisation of the Suez Canal Company. Months of argument and recrimination were followed by the brief and violent conflict—in the Canal Zone— between Egypt, Israel, France and Great Britain. One result of the conflict was the blocking of the Suez Canal and it appeared that it might remain indefinitely out of use. Finally, more sensible counsels prevailed and the Canal was formally re-opened in June 1975.

The Canal is some 60 miles long (including the stretches which pass through the Bitter Lakes) and it is punctuated at its two ends and at its centre by the three considerable towns of Port Said, Suez and Ismailia. None of these towns is on the present tourist trail and with the reduction in sea passenger travel fewer and fewer people will have the opportunity of making their acquaintance during the Canal passage. For many decades Port Said was a familiar port of call. Statues of Lesseps and Queen Victoria dominated the main breakwater and it was almost obligatory to land and do one's shopping at the legendary Simon Artz. Seriously damaged in the fighting of 1956, Port Said was never a place of any attraction; its most imposing building was the headquarters administration building of the Canal Company itself.

Nor has the town of Suez anything to attract the traveller. Before 1967 it had a museum of a not very distinguished kind. The 1967 war caused its closure and the destruction of a large part of the town; one would like to hope the opportunity will be taken to build a better Suez. If one had to choose between the three towns, the choice would certainly be Ismailia. This too suffered from the 1967 war and here also the museum—a more pretentious affair than Suez—has been closed since 1967. But Ismailia is, or was, agreeably laid out and has the advantage of being pleasantly situated on the shore of Lake Timsah, one of the Bitter Lakes aiding the route of the Canal.

Across the Canal is the Egyptian province of Sinai, still at the time of writing in the military occupation of the State of Israel. Kantara situated on the Canal between Port Said and Ismailia has been the traditional crossing place from Africa to Asia and not far from it is the site of the ancient Pelusium, the traditional fortress town guardian of the Eastern marches of Egypt.

The province of Sinai which in geographical shape is another and larger Delta is a region of mountain and desert owing its celebrity to the Old Testament story of the Israelites in the time of Moses. For the tourist, when access to it was possible, it provided one interesting, if rather elaborate, excursion, the Monastery of St Catherine. This is situated in the southern portion of the Sinai peninsula in close proximity to the two most famous mountains of Sinai, the Mount of Moses and the Mount of St Catherine, both some 7,000 feet in height. The Mount of Moses, as its name implies, was the mountain where traditionally Moses received the Tables of the Law; the Mount of St Catherine was the mountain where the body of St Catherine, martyred at Alexandria, was transported by the angels.

Her monastery is remarkable in Egypt as not being a Coptic foundation. It was founded in the sixth century by the Byzantine emperor Justinian and has always remained faithful to the Orthodox faith. Though not so ancient as the monasteries of the Wadi Natroun, it is clear from travellers' descriptions that it is place of much greater interest. Buildings, mosaics and paintings, museum, library are all noteworthy. Its library indeed was sufficiently noteworthy to attract the attention of nineteenth-century collectors; its most famous treasure was purloined not too honestly for the Czar Alexander II of Russia; but the Soviet government in the 1930s decided that they did not want it any longer; it was thrown on the world market; an English subscription, largely inspired by the Archbishop of Canterbury, was raised; and it now reposes in the British Museum under the name of Codex Sinaiticus. Even deprived of this treasure, the library of St Catherine is said to be, after the Vatican, the most interesting and valuable Christian library in the world.

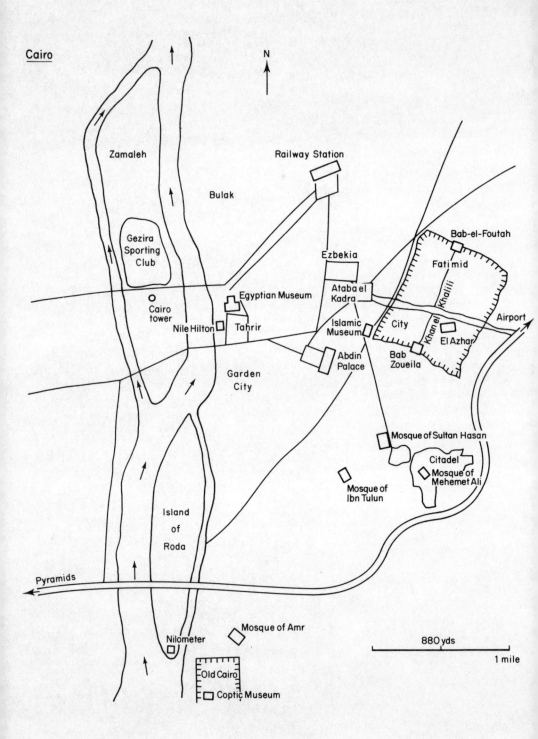

Cairo

N

Zamaleh

Bulak

Railway Station

Gezira
Sporting
Club

Ezbekia

Bab-el-Foutah

Cairo
tower

Egyptian Museum

Ataba el
Kadra

Fatimid

Khan el Khalili

Airport

Nile Hilton

Tahrir

Islamic
Museum

City

El Azhar

Abdin
Palace

Bab
Zoueila

Garden
City

Mosque of Sultan Hasan

Citadel

Island
of
Roda

Mosque of
Ibn Tulun

Mosque of
Mehemet Ali

Pyramids

Nilometer

Mosque of Amr

880 yds

1 mile

Old Cairo

Coptic Museum

6 CAIRO

As the aeroplane makes its descent over the twinkling lights of the Delta, one becomes aware of a greater light rapidly revealing itself as a vast area of concentrated illumination, the capital of Egypt. Arriving by daylight one gets the full impression of the vast inhabited sprawling urban zone. Yet the airport is at its north eastern periphery close to the modern suburb of Heliopolis. As one drives into the city—and it is a longish drive—one soon encounters the enduring impressions of the city, crowded traffic, blaring horns, struggling pedestrians, incoherent buildings, the haze of dust. Two impressions which have not endured from a generation ago are, first, the all-pervading smell, a compound of oriental humanity, oriental spices and decaying rubbish, and, secondly, the circling kites, sinister black birds which traditionally hovered over the city and gave to everything a sense of finality and death.

The airport bus threads the north-eastern suburbs. Houses with gardens, sometimes of pretension, but now traffic-ridden and dust-covered, line the bumpy carriage-way. The suburbs insensibly give way to town. The bus-driver if knowledgeable will take the opportunity of escaping from the urban mesh by turning southwards onto the highway which in a sense by-passes the modern conurbation. It does not by-pass the whole city for while on the right one is conscious of the city of the living, one becomes conscious on the left of the City of the Dead. This is one of the extraordinary zones of vast extent which for centuries has been the cemetery of the Moslems. And rightly called a city because among the countless thousands of the tombs are countless thousands of living humans beings. This zone which we must visit in due course is so built over with the tombs of the departed, sometimes of enormous size, that it resembles less a cemetery than a sprawling desert town. It is called for some reason the Tombs of the Caliphs.

Almost immediately beyond, one's attention is seized on the right-hand size by enormous walls and battlements on an adjacent hill. This is the back view of the Citadel and in a city where one comes to pray for landmarks it is much the most prominent landmark. This also we shall visit. Skirting the Citadel, our highway turns westward and skirting on the left another City of the Dead (this time called the Tombs of the Mamelukes) it hits the modern city broadside on, crosses the main street called the Sharia Abou Sefein and reaches the waterside. This is the small eastern branch of the Nile which encloses the Island of Roda.

We are now in a southern prolongation of the City. If we were to go straight on, we would cross the Isle of Roda, cross the Nile by the large bridge called Koulry el Guiza (the Giza Bridge) and find ourselves in the suburb of Giza and on the road to the Pyramids. But pausing at our first contact with the Nile, we can briefly take geographical stock. Though we have crossed the southern pro- longation of Cairo, we have by no means reached its southern tip. To the south of us are still the original Arab quarters once called Fustat with the first mosque, the mosque of Amr; and further still is 'Old Cairo', the Christian quarter with its ancient Coptic churches. But the vast bulk of the city is to the west and north. Beyond the Nile and stretching north from Giza are the vast building deve- lopments of the twentieth century. Roda island itself is covered with buildings. North of it Gezira or Zameleh, another and larger island, has long been incorporated in the city complex but mercifully preserves on its southern half a large open area occupied by parks, racecourse, polo ground and the once-famous Gezira Sporting Club.

But we have still not taken in the city proper. This lies im- mediately to our north. Compressed to begin with between the Citadel and the river, it expands as it goes northwards into an ever-increasing bulk finally stretching out north-eastwards to Abassia and Heliopolis whence we have come and north-westwards to Bulak, once its river port and Shubra, once its elegant Khedivial suburb.

A more likely and much more daunting approach from the airport takes one right through the centre of the city. This is achieved by modern streets cutting through the mediaeval maze to make direct for the European quarter. These streets fail unhappily to achieve any expectation. Drawn on a nineteenth-century or early twentieth- century scale, they are quite inadequate for the press of traffic of modern times. Nor do they provide worthwhile urban scenery. An endless vista of semi-European, semi-Oriental buildings in every stage of dirt or dilapidation is one's only impression. Only occas- ionally can one have a surprising vista, for example the Mosque of El-Azhar which suddenly on the left proclaims its existence (sometimes in English). After a long struggle the bus reaches the open space called Midan-el-Ataba-el-Kadra, a key point in the city plan.

This was, until the modernisation of Cairo began, the city's western limit. To the right and immediately north west of it is the Ezbekia Square to which we shall return, for it was in the nineteenth and early twentieth century the effective centre of Cairo. But our main street continues, no longer now through the mediaeval maze but through rectilineal street crossings; bends right and takes us into the city's modern centre, the Midan-el-Tahrir or Independence Square.

This is a modern creation and, considering the amount of work that must have been entailed, the result is disappointing. The Blue Guide describes it unkindly, but not unfairly, as a *tohu bohu de voitures et d'autobus.* The square is situated close to, but not on, the Nile and one could be unaware of the existence of the river. In the old days the view was obstructed by the large mass of the Kasr-el-Nil barracks familiar to generations of British soldiers. This has now been demolished and replaced by the Hilton Hotel which, with its western entrance facing directly on the Nile, may be taken as the city's second landmark. We have now reached the river at a point some two miles north of our other journey and are facing not the Island of Roda but the Island of Zamaleh which we can reach by the Kasr-el-Nil bridge now renamed Tahrir. Separating us on our left hand side from our previous stopping-point is the so-called Garden City stretching along the riverside of the Nile.

So inadequate an account of an approach-arrival may give some idea of the geographical dimensions of the city, but it hardly does justice to its human dimensions. For Cairo in the last few decades has suffered the fate which now seems inevitable for the capital cities of countries which one calls 'underdeveloped.' In the sophisticated worlds of London and New York whole central areas are evacuated to become ghettoes or empty deserts. In the poverty-stricken worlds of Cairo, and Mexico City and Calcutta, the population piles into the centre to a breaking point which somehow is never reached. The Cairo population figures are remorselessly recorded: in Bonaparte's time 200,000; by 1927 a million; two million in 1950; four million in 1967; probably six or seven million in 1980. It is not necessary to dilate too much upon the causes: the high birth rate; the medical advances which have reduced the death rate; the mechanisation of agriculture (and there must be much more to come); the lure of the city lights to impoverished villagers; with the added element in the troubled history of Egypt of those forcibly displaced by the military operations of recent years in the Canal Zone.

The result of all this on the central areas of Cairo is not difficult to imagine. It must now, demographically speaking, be one of the most crowded areas in the world. But the crowds are not only in the habitations. Rising living standards have done their work and have transformed the conditions in the streets. A generation ago the Cairo sheik or merchant, honking his way through the streets in his chauffeur-driven Cadillac, had a comparatively easy passage. In the era of small cars at popular prices he is totally submerged in a swarm of wildly competing vehicles which the police at the principal street crossings desperately strive to control. The problem is not confined to the moving vehicles. Parking space is at a premium and the city authorities have long given up the battle of the city pavements. Almost every available square yard is occupied by a parked car. The word 'almost' is intentional; in the sad run-down which has beset certain aspects of modern Egypt the city authorities have not kept up with necessary repairs; every few yards there are holes or excavations which could break a human ankle or the back axle of an automobile.

This situation has serious results for the visitor who likes to visit foreign cities on foot. Along some of the Nile boulevards, notwithstanding the constant hoot and hum of traffic, it is possible to walk with some comfort. Inland from the Nile countless Egyptians do in fact negotiate the streets on foot. But it is not a thing that anyone would now do from choice. The sad fact is that large parts of Cairo are for practical purposes impracticable for the would-be pedestrians among the visitors.

How then to visit this most fascinating of cities? The visitor is thrown back on the tourist coach, the hired car and the Arabic-speaking guide. It is always congenial to do a riverside drive, the Nile provides miles of so-called Corniche and an agreeable diversion may be made to Gezira on the southern half of Zamaleh island. Here is the city's third landmark, the Cairo Tower. Forging inland into the city centre one will start inevitably from Independence Square. Bounding this on the north is one of Cairo's major tourist-spots, the Egyptian Museum. From the Square one can do a quadrilateral of other squares. North-eastwards from behind the Egyptian Museum two wide streets lead to the Railway Station, an unlikely object it might seem for a tourist visit. But the antecedent square, a favourite rendezvous for Cairo's political moments, now contains an imposing statue of Rameses II brought here in 1952 from Memphis; and the railway station itself possesses, for those who are intersted in such things, a remarkable museum of the Egyptian Railways, traditionally one of the most progressive of Egyptian organisations.

From the station square one may go southwards along a street which, unlike most Cairo streets, has been allowed to retain its traditional name—Clot Bey. This leads to the Ezbekia which, as already stated, long formed the western fringe of the ancient city. Most of it until the nineteenth century was a lake or at any rate became so during the annual inundation of the Nile which, no respecter of cities, often covered considerable areas of Cairo itself. Bonaparte made his headquarters here in the palace of a Sheikh. The ambitious Ismail decided that it should be the centre of his Europeanised Cairo. The lake was laid out as a garden; a statue of Ibrahim Pasha was erected; an opera house was built in honour of the opening of the Suez Canal; and just off it there flourished until comparatively modern times the famous Shepheards, the hotel par excellence of every self-respecting visitor to Egypt. The Ezbekia has alas fallen from its high estate. Shepheards was burnt down in the riots of the 1950s and the Opera was burnt down by accident in 1971. Shepheards was rebuilt on a new site on the Nile Corniche. Of the traditional Ezbekia only the ageing Hotel Continentale remains.

Continuing our route southwards we proceed to the large Gomhoureya (Revolution) Square in front of the Abdin Palace. The Abdin Palace was bought in the nineteenth century from a Pasha of that name by the Khedive Ismail and was made by him into the principal royal palace of Cairo. For a few years after the fall of Farouk it was on public view and one hopes it might be so again. Internally it exhibited the gloomy grandeur of the very de luxe nineteenth-century hotel. Clearly the royal family had not stinted itself on its decoration. Innumerable family portraits hung on interminable walls. Innumerable suites of French furniture filled the rooms. The most distinguished part of the furnishings were the brocades, again principally French, which must have been ordered in Paris by the acre rather than the square yard. 'Ismail Pasha', wrote Lord Cromer, 'added about £7,000,000 a year for thirteen years to the debt of Egypt…. The whole of the borrowed money, except £16,000,000 spent on the Suez Canal, was squandered.' Perhaps the brocades were part of the squandering.

We finish our quadrilateral by turning west and returning to Tahrir. But we ought not to dismiss the European quarter without sampling its two principal streets, the Suleiman Pasha (now re-christened Talaat Harb) and Kasr-el-Nil. These intersect at a square also once called Suleiman Pasha and adorned with a statue of that dignitary who in historical truth was a Frenchman called Capitaine de Sèves, the reorganiser of the army of Mehemet Ali. These are the streets of the banks and tourist-agencies and here will be found the shops for those who like to buy expensive European articles in Oriental cities. Nor does this area exhaust what might be called the European developments of Cairo. There is a wide diversity of museums — Ethnography, Geology, Fine Arts, Civilisation, Egyptian Sculpture, Modern Art, Agriculture, Botanic Garden, and on the island of Roda is the Manyal Palace. And on the far side of the Nile, before Giza, can be found what is said to be an excellent Zoo.

Even before the Great 'European' expansion of modern times Cairo was one of the world's most complicated cities. But it is possible with the aid of a good plan to take it, so to speak, to pieces and see how it all happened. The original reason for it, as for the ancient capital of Memphis a few miles to the South, was obviously its situation at the point where the Nile Valley expands into the Delta. The Romans, when they arrived, did not apparently Romanise Memphis; instead they built a military camp at what is now the southern end of Cairo which acquired the name of Babylon. No further development took place in Roman or Byzantine times, but Babylon still survives under the name of Old Cairo.

Babylon came into history in 641 AD when the Arab army under its leader Amr laid siege. After the capture of the fortress Amr erected beside it, allegedly on the actual site of his tent, the mosque which, though repeatedly rebuilt, still bears his name. To the north and east of Babylon the Arabs simultaneously built the town called Fustat, which was the real foundation of the modern city, and to the north of Fustat the Umaiyad dynasty in the following century built the quarter of Askar. The next addition, again to the north-east (and immediately west of the present Citadel) was the quarter of Ibn Tulun. Of these three additions to the original Babylon remarkably little survives, much the most notable relic being the great mosque of Ibn Tulun.

A more permanent foundation was that of the Fatimid dynasty in the tenth century. By them a self-contained walled city was built, again to the north-east of the previous extensions. Much of this recognisably survives, notably the north and south walls and the three great gates called Bab-el-Foutah, Bab-an-Nasr and Bab-Zoueila. It was this last foundation which, strangely, gave the city its modern name; the general of the Fàtimid Caliph named it El-Kahira or 'the Victorious One' and by Europeans it was easily corrupted into Cairo. The true Arab name is Misr.

In the twelfth century Cairo faced the challenge of the Crusades. As a defensive measure the unfortified town of Fustat was burnt and thus passed out of history. Cairo proper was successfully defended by Saladin who became one of its greatest rulers. It was by the genius of Saladin that Cairo received its most spectacular addition, the Citadel. Saladin's ambition, never wholly achieved, was to enclose the whole city in an extension of the Fatimid walls; by contrast he did complete the impressive fortifications of the Citadel.

In the following century began the rule of the Mamelukes, slaves of Circassian origin who by an astonishing succession of assassinations and uprisings established a chain of rulers who maintained themselves until the appearance of the all-conquering Turks. No political system could be conceived which would be less conducive to the development of a great city or the creation of great works of architecture; in fact the two and a half centuries of the Mamelukes witnessed an enormous expansion particularly to the south and west of the Fatimid city (the population in the mid-fourteenth century is said to have been 500,000) and the foundation of countless mosques and other buildings which have made Cairo the finest mediaeval city in the world. It was the Turkish conquest in 1517 which brought decline; some ornamental buildings of the Turkish period do survive but the population steadily reduced and it was only with Mehemet Ali that the city awoke once more.

This account of the successive extensions of the city is hardly intelligible without reference to the governing facts of weather and water. Cities are prone to expand in the direction of the prevailing wind and in Cairo the prevailing wind is north. The deviation to the north-east resulted from the course of the Canal called the Khalig which started from the Nile opposite Roda and flowed north-eastwards to the Delta. The successive urban developments closely bordered the right bank of the Canal. The Nile itself in mediaeval times had a course far to the east of its present course and when it changed its channel a special port had to be built which still survives opposite Gezira under the name of Bulac.

Mehemet Ali was responsible for the construction of what has ever since been the most spectacular building of Cairo, the Mehemet Ali mosque on the citadel. Apart from this he did not transform the city as he transformed his chosen capital of Alexandria. The

Europeanisation of Cairo came in the later nineteenth century with Ismail. It was Ismail who planned and launched the European quarter and brought Cairo into the modern age. He also laid hands on the ancient city. From the citadel a straight wide street called after Mehemet Ali, but now re-named El-Kálaa, was driven from the Citadel through the ancient quarters to our key-point square of Ataba-el-Kadra. From this square also two parallel streets were driven eastwards through the heart of the Fatimid city; the El Azhar street by which we have travelled from the airport and the parallel Muski leading to the bazaars. It was not till later in the nineteenth century that the Khalig canal was tackled. This had become Cairo's main sewer with a stench so horrendous that Europeans used to wonder how people could inhabit the adjacent houses and survive. It was eventually filled in and the main street now called Sharia Port Said built on its site.

So large are Cairo's Europeanised quarters that one could live there for years without being aware that the city had anything older than a nineteenth-century past and for those who are frail or squeamish there is much to be said for remaining as close as possible to the Nile-side and admiring the ever-fascinating, ever-changing views. The more adventurous character who wishes to see the ancient Cairo faces a daunting programme. It is necessary to begin somewhere and historically the best start is Old Cairo.

This, as we have seen, is at the City' southern extremity and demands a conveyance. It takes one to a strange small enclosed world which one can still imagine as the Roman Babylon. Parts of the Roman walls survive; within, the Roman fortress has become a small fortress of ancient Christianity.

Two Roman towers are identifiable in the Western wall and on the south side can be seen the two projections which framed the grand Roman entrance. One can get also some idea of the astonishing changes of levels that can be produced on sites which are inhabited through the centuries. Jews and Greek Orthodox have staked their claims in this small area and one may find both a synagogue and a Greek Orthodox church. But primarily Old Cairo is the fortress of the Copts. We encountered the Copts at Alexandria and clearly Alexandria was their first headquarters. It is impossible, even if one wishes to do so, to know the details of Coptic history after the Arab takeover. At first, as we have seen, the conquerors were accepted, even welcomed. But through the centuries, with the changing Arab governments and successive revolutions, with the Crusades and with the Turks, the Copts must have undergone every variety of experience. The main thing that is clear is that, due doubtless to the persisting proselytising of Islam, the religion of the Copts, from being almost universal in the country, became that of a small minority. The wonder, when one looks at the other countries of North Africa, is that they survived at all; in the twentieth century they number perhaps 5% of the total population of Egypt. The second thing that is clear is that the Coptic religion, suddenly subjected in the seventh century to the rule of an alien faith and sundered simultaneously from the rest of Christianity, became, so to speak, frozen in its seventh-century form. The services are still conducted in the now unintelligible Coptic language, though sometimes with an Arabic translation; the Coptic doctrine has been described as in a permanent state of 'deathlike lethargy'; and no new fashions have taken over in Coptic architecture. The third thing that is clear is that at some period the Copts, following the example of the Arabs, removed their Headquarters from Alexandria to Cairo. The Patriarch's residence is in the north-western part of the city near the modern cathedral of St Mark in the street along which we have already passed called Clot Bey. Historically Old Cairo encloses the oldest Coptic traditions.

These begin with the Church of Abu Sarga and with the tradition that it was in the crypt of this church that the Virgin and Child spent a month after their flight to Egypt. The Church itself is thought to be a reconstruction of the tenth century and provides the model of most Coptic churches. At the entrance end is a narthex or vestibule containing in one corner a baptistery. From it three openings through a wooden screen lead into the main nave and two side aisles. These lead up to the sanctuary, the aisles having galleries and the nave a pointed roof. Wooden screens also close off the sanctury at the end of the nave and the two side chapels which terminate the aisles. From the side chapels steps descend to the crypt where one will be quick to observe that the columns date from Greek or Roman times.

The Coptic churches contain little enough that one could classify as works of art. In Abu Sarga some of the carvings on the screens are noteworthy. If interest is sufficiently aroused to look at other Coptic churches in this little area, one can find a few good carvings and paintings in the nearby church of St Barbara; and in El-Muallaga, sometimes called the Hanging Church, is a remarkable mosaic pulpit reminiscent of the tenth century in Southern Italy. This last church is remarkable as being built actually on top of the grand Roman entrance which we have already noticed and the vaults of which can be visited from the Coptic Museum.

The Coptic Museum has been one of the happier inspirations of modern Cairo. Privately founded in 1910, it was subsequently taken over by the State and the sensible decision was made to concentrate here all the Christian antiquities of Cairo. The result is impressive. Displayed in some thirty rooms are the remarkable manifestations of Coptic art through the centuries, sculpture, capitals, bas-reliefs, funerary steles, frescoes, paintings, textiles, embroideries, icons, innumerable wood carvings; then metal work, marbles, pottery and even manuscripts. The contents are not more remarkable than the setting; the museum fits itself into a small area, with attractive gardens and courtyards. Above all in this deafening city, it breathes an air of peace.

Only the most determined sightseer would drag himself away from this to visit the nearby mosque of Amr. This is the oldest Moslem foundation of Cairo built as we have seen immediately after the Arab conquest and immediately to the north of Babylon. But this mosque has been so frequently rebuilt that its interest in truth is historical rather than architectural or artistic.

There is also the opportunity at Old Cairo to visit the Nilometer. This is at the south tip of the island of Roda less than half a mile to the west, but it unfortunately requires a detour to cross the narrow arm of the Nile. The Nilometer is also one of Cairo's most ancient monuments dating, it is alleged, from the year 716 AD. For centuries it was also Cairo's most vital monument, registering as it did the all-important levels which measured the annual inundation of the Nile. The octagonal column with its measurements can still be seen; no more, alas, is the annual celebration when the irrigation could be started and the whole city turned out to see the ceremonial cutting of the dyke on the river's eastern bank.

To see the Moslem wonders of Cairo it is best to start with the favourite tourist round and to visit the mosques of El-Azhar, Ibn Tulun, Sultan Hassan and Mehemet Ali. The El-Azhar mosque which we have already noticed is in the middle of the Fatimid city; founded by the Fatimids in the year 970 AD as a mosque, it was shortly after made also a university with the object of propagating the Shia doctrine of Islam to which the Fatimids subscribed. On the expulsion of the Fatimids the university obviously was suppressed, but it was reopened in the thirteenth century as a university now for propagating the Sunni doctrine of Orthodox Mahomedanism. In the ensuing centuries the El-Azhar has become the intellectual, doctrinal and spiritual centre of the whole Moslem world. 'For a thousand years the Centre of a Thousand Million Moslems' it has been known proudly to proclaim. It is without doubt one of the most important institutions in the world.

Not much of its educational activity is on view to the tourist, though the students are numbered up to 20,000. Sometimes as one penetrates through the elaborate entrance into the main courtyard of the mosque one becomes aware of a group earnestly following the discourse of a teacher; more often one is struck by the sight of individual students seated alone and apparently repeating interminably the truths which it is their duty to learn. The needs of the university have visibly conflicted with the concept of the mosque and architecturally speaking we do not see the perfection we shall find elsewhere in Cairo. But the main design is clear enough, the great open court leading to the great hall or Liwan with the forest of columns upholding it and containing the necessary Moslem elements of Mihrab and Minbar. The construction is largely of that type which becomes so familiar in countries where Islam took over from Greeks and Romans; we become aware of a forest of columns (there are well over 200 in all) supporting the hall and of the fact that most of them visibly are antique Greek or Roman brought here higgledy piggledy with little attempt at matching in height or style, those which were too short being propped up with supports and those which were too tall being cut down. There is a similar discordance among the capitals. And there is an endless fascination in wandering through this forest, gazing at column after column and wondering from what ancient buildings they came.

Our next visit—Ibn Tulun—could hardly be a greater contrast; there is nothing haphazard or higgledy piggledy here. Ibn Tulun is the most professional of architectural jobs and a building of quite extraordinary ambition. And yet it is older than El-Azhar—its traditional date is 876 AD; it is in fact, next to the mosque of Amr, the oldest Moslem foundation in the city. The scale is staggering; it covers more than six acres. No less striking is the symmetry; by contrast with El-Azhar one enters at the corner of the prayer mosque and through the forest of pillars (no longer columns here) one looks out upon the full immensity of the main courtyard. One could believe here the first tradition of Islam, that the object of a mosque is to provide space for all its followers. It is not less impressive as the tourist generally sees it; completely empty with the exception of the small central feature which is obligatory upon all mosques, the water basin and washing place surmounted here

by a small but elegant dome. Surrounding it as we stand with our
backs to the prayer-mosque are the three lesser liwans or colonnades;
but again not built with columns but with pillars. The secret of
the construction is that the entire scheme is built of brick, but the
whole of the brick is covered with a white plaster—and the
apparently endless series of white plaster columns is deeply impressive. Totally similar is the prayer mosque itself, though here
the pillars are ranged in five rows instead of two; totally central
also are the mihrab and the minbar exactly pointed as they should
be towards Mecca. There is nothing very lofty about prayer mosque
or colonnades; what are remarkable as we gaze upwards are the
identical pointed arches which throughout the building constitute
the architecture between each pair of pillars; arches not Gothic in
any western understanding of the term but delicately moulded
into rhythmic lines which culminate in a point at the top. It would
be interesting to know who was the architect of this astonishing
creation; the cognoscenti will not go further than saying learnedly
that the design is of Mesopotamian type, transported perhaps as it
were bodily into the alien soil of Egypt.

   If one were determined to be critical, the criticism might be
that the whole effect is soulless. The white plaster, above the level
of the pillars, is intricately carved with surface mouldings; the
expertise is staggering but the monotony is overwhelming also.
What really saves the building is the minaret placed in the dead
centre of the colonnade facing the prayer mosque and apparently
added after the completion of the building. Its charming, un-
assuming whiteness and its visible winding stairway invite inspection
and the temptation should not be resisted. A modest climb takes
one onto the flat roof of the liwan or colonnade so that one can
gaze down on the great courtyard and the prayer mosque beyond.
But the reward is not only the internal view, one can see the quarters
outside. By no means Cairo's greatest view, this yet includes the
pyramids to the west and the citadel to the east and below the
citadel the great minarets of our next visit, Sultan Hasan.

   Sultan Hasan provides a second contrast; nothing could be less
like either Ibn Tulun or El-Azhar. We approach it through the
high buildings lining the new (Mehemet Ali) street which Ismail
drove from the Citadel to Ataba el Kadra; we dismount before
an implacable precipice of grey stone; we climb some stone steps
and enter through a gigantic Gothic archway 85 feet high. The
corridor twists and turns in the darkness before projecting us
suddenly into the central court. This is, by comparison with Ibn

Tulun, quite small; the problem, as we shall see, was how to fit a great building into an essentially limited site. In Ibn Tulun the overwhelming impression is horizontal; in Sultan Hasan the overwhelming impression is vertical. The courtyard is completely square; an ablution fountain, as required, in the centre; at the end the prayer mosque. The stupendous effect is produced by the architecture of the four walls of the courtyard. Four more gigantic Gothic stone archways open through them into the arms of the building, the archway on the prayer-mosque side even larger than its fellows. Beyond the prayer-mosque the Sultan has his mausoleum under a dome a hundred feet high; at the mosque's southern extremity rises the highest minaret in Cairo. The foundation dates from 1360 AD and from the outset was intended as a 'school mosque' or madrasa. Inserted into the corners of the architecture are still the halls and schoolrooms for the various Moslem studies. No question here of rivalling El-Azhar; there was nothing universal about Sultan Hasan; it was essentially a school for Cairo. If Moslem scholars could be made by architecture, this was the way to do it; Sultan Hasan is on the plane of York and Lincoln and of Northern France.

To visit our fourth mosque it is necessary to make the steep climb up to the immediately adjacent Citadel. This, as we have seen, was built by Saladin and is on an extensive scale; if it was all on view, a half day would be required. What can be seen are the imposing entrance gateway added in the eighteenth century; the small mosque of An-Nasir built in the fourteenth century; and the ancient well, known as Joseph's Well, on which the Citadel depended and which still exists to a depth of 300 feet. Mehemet Ali destroyed the original castle of the ruler or governor, but constructed instead the Gohara or Bijou Palace which was one of the most entrancing of Cairene delights. Built on a comparatively modest scale, it was decorated almost entirely in *trompe d'oeil.* Alas that this pretty building a few years ago was damaged by fire. Not merely has it not been rebuilt and restored, the wreckage of the fire has not even been cleared up. Its present state is a reproach to the authorities of Cairo.

But what we have come to see is Mehemet Ali's mosque. Mehemet Ali provides a third contrast: nothing could be less like Sultan Hasan or Ibn Tulun or El-Azhar. We are here in the presence of the Turkish tradition, the tradition which, deriving from the Byzantine Santa Sophia in Constantinople, was continued in that city by the first Turkish conquerors in such famous buildings as the Suleimanye and the Blue Mosque and became stylised in the later centuries as the only architecturally permissible design. Here are no ancient columns, no plastered brick pillars, no gigantic stone arches; here everything is subordinated to the single impressive feature, the gigantic central dome. This, as in the older examples, requires four semi-domes, and at the angles four smaller domes, and the whole thing is perfectly worked out. Without being on the scale of Constantinople, Mehemet Ali's effort is impressively large. The courtyard and the ablution fountain are there, the prayer-mosque has its mihrab and its minbar, the symmetry is perfectly maintained. In one arm of the building beneath a cupola supported by four square pillars is Mehemet Ali's own impressive tomb.

The mosque is sometimes called the Alabaster Mosque for its walls are largely faced with alabaster from Beni Suef. This is the first thing which makes a strikingly different effect from anything we have so far seen. The second thing is the decoration; we are freed here from the merciless monotony of abstract decor which is the speciality of Islam. The architect was European and one likes to think he had imbibed the virtues of the more human epochs of Europe. One looks at the detail and the general effect and wonders whether one dare say rococo or baroque. Whatever it is, it is very inexpressive of everything one knows about Mehemet Ali. Perhaps one would have to say a pastiche, but one which reflects the highest credit on an architect of the early nineteenth century. His bit of bad luck was the clock, a singularly tasteless effort which had to be mounted as the central feature of the liwan opposite the prayer-mosque, for it was presented by Mehemet Ali's principal European patron King Louis Philippe of France.

The ultimate treat of the Citadel is the view from the terrace immediately behind the mosque. The Tombs of the Caliphs, the City of the Dead which we passed on our first arrival, are hidden from us by the Citadel walls; instead we look out westwards and northwards through the inevitable haze of dust upon the immense urban panorama of the modern and mediaeval quarters. Miles away to the west, the pyramids stand out enormous against the horizon and preferably against the setting sun; nearer one can trace the course of the Nile and appreciate the tremendous jumble of modern buildings through which it makes its way. Swinging right-handed, the eye loses the sky-scrapers and encounters the minarets. Immediately below us are the lofty minarets of Sultan Hasan; thence extending northwards the astonishing architectural forest which traces the successive extensions of the mediaeval town. The effect is overwhelming, defying any comment except perhaps that of an English poet writing of another Egyptian vision: 'Gaze on my works, ye mortals, and despair.'

The challenge of Moslem Cairo is formidable, but three forays might be suggested to the beginner, the City of the Dead, the Khan-el-Khalili and the Fatimid City. The City of the Dead, miscalled the Tombs of the Caliphs, lies as we have seen behind the Citadel. The skyscape from the road which we first traversed is sensational; a closer visit is daunting. It is a city indeed with streets, squares, houses, even shops but it is simultaneously a cemetery and simultaneously a rubbish heap. No use here to tell the visitor where his car should drive and how to make the tour; the piles of rubbish soon bring to a halt any wheeled vehicle and for a close appreciation of the great monuments the last stretch must be done painfully on foot. The highlights are the Tomb of Sultan Barkuk and the Tomb of Kaitbey. These are both of the fifteenth century, that is to say, in the midst of that period of turbulence and ruthlessness that was the history of mediaeval Cairo. Both tombs are very large, designed clearly with a view to permanent upkeep by a permanent staff. The two domes of Sultan Barkuk are outstanding and impressive, the first in Egypt, one is told, that were built entirely of stone. The minaret also is impressive and outstanding, starting as it does from a cubical base to ascend first from a square to an octagon and then from an octagon to a cylinder. To wander about the interior is to experience the sensations of a small Oriental palace, silent and deserted as it now is. But it is also like a mosque with the central court and the four Liwans, with the prayer-mosque facing south-east towards Mecca. The Sultan has his mausoleum in the north-east corner of the building; his wives occupy the matching corner on the other side.

Kaitbey is a later work (about 1480 AD) but is probably the finest in the City of the Dead. The detail everywhere is exquisite; the external view with the soaring minaret is one of the most successful in Cairo; within the soaring lines of the tomb-chamber are immensely impressive. Both these great monuments have the advantage, so lacking in the Old City itself, of being detached from their surroundings and thus capable of being appreciated as architectural wholes.

It is not possible within the scope of a single chapter to see much of the Old City, but two preliminary visits may be essayed. The first must be the tourist's favourite, along the Muski to the

great Khan-el-Khalili Bazaar. Most of this excursion, notwithstanding the deterrents, must be done on foot. The car can take
one to Ataba-el-Kadra and some way along the Muski street;
arrived at the line of the Fatimid walls it is better to dismount. We
are now walking parallel with the new El-Azhar Street along which
we came and are striking east across the Fatimid city until we
reach the cross street with the Kasaba (now called Mouizz din Allah)
which was the main north to south city thoroughfare in Fatimid
times. The bazaar is situated immediately on the left beyond this
crossing and is said to have been built in the fourteenth century
on the site of the Fatimid palace. It presents itself now as a maze of
bewildering lanes crowded with stalls and people in which one
can pleasantly lose oneself for half an hour. Sadly it must be admitted
that in these days there is little to buy; much of the merchandise is
European or machine-made. But it is fascinating to watch the
occasional craftsman still hammering out his brass or working his
inlay and it is fascinating too to see how the trades are segregated
in the Eastern manner. Purchases of real value can be made in the
goldsmith's quarter and the enterprising European housewife can
spend a happy half-hour among the spices.

The second visit should be to explore the Kasaba street itself.
Before doing so it may be well to mention some of the things to
look for. First, obviously the mosques, whether of congregational
or Madrasah types. Secondly, the street fountains. Thirdly, the
occasional surviving hammams or public baths. Fourthly, the Islamic
private houses often with their lattice-work windows once so typical
of Cairo. Last but not least the caravanserais, the 'inns of the East';
great courtyards surrounded with stables and sleeping quarters
and everything needed by those arrived from a long desert trek.

The length of the Kasaba is slightly over a mile and it must
necessarily be done on foot; the best plan is for the car to drop one
at the northern gate and pick one up at the southern. The northern
gate is the Bab-el-Foutah and it is worth more than a passing glance.
Built about 1100 AD, its design is both simple and massive, depend-
ing for its effect on the fine ashlar stonework of which it is built. A
stretch of Fatimid wall runs south-eastwards hence to the next
equally impressive gate, Bab-en-Nasr, and the walk is worth making,
if possible, along the top of the city wall. The wall bounds the
great enclosure of the congregational mosque of Hakim built by
the caliph of that name about 1000 AD; it is our first visit on the
left after passing through the Bab-el-Foutah and though now partly
ruinous is of interest as being one of the few surviving Fatimid

buildings of Cairo. As we continue on our way we begin to get the full flavour of Oriental Cairo. Narrow lanes diverge to right and left often with tempting vistas, but we must resist temptation. It would take weeks, months, years to ferret out and identify all the mediaeval relics and Fatimid city is only one of the quarters of mediaeval Cairo. But very close to us down one of the left-hand lanes is a worthwhile excursion to see the Bet-es-Souhaymi, an interesting survival of the Turkish period, for it is an amalgam of two seventeenth- and eighteenth-century houses with much of the exterior decoration intact and well preserved inside the traditional arrangement of Oriental living. Again on the left is the small mosque of Aqmar dating from the eleventh century and preserving its Fatimid façade; and a hundred yards beyond it the relics of the palace of the Emir Bechtaq built by a sultan's brother-in-law in AD 1334.

There follows on the right a very grand sequence of mediaeval architecture. First, the madrasa or school-mosque of the Sultan Barkuk whose tomb we have visited in the City of the Dead. Less grand than the Hasan mosque, it exhibits nevertheless some of the same characteristics, notably a splendid and beautiful portal and an imposing courtyard. Secondly, the mausoleum of An-Nasir whose mosque we have noticed in the Citadel and is thus of fourteenth-century date; the minaret is intact, but sadly much of the building is gone for his reign, we are told, was the greatest epoch of Cairene mediaeval art. Thirdly, the mausoleum of Kalaoun dating from the previous century. This is a large compound of buildings, comprising not only the mausoleum, but also a madrasa-mosque and a hospital. The splendid street façade is suggestive of the Crusaders or the Normans. The massive minaret surmounts the north-east angle of the tomb and is worth climbing for the view. A great entrance doorway gives access both to madrasa and mausoleum; in both is to be seen a beautiful mihrab. The tomb-chamber, solemn and imposing, is said to be inspired by Armenian traditions and by the Dome of the Rock in Jerusalem. Back in the street the façade faces a number of ancient buildings including one of Turkish date.

We are now passing on the left the exterior of the Khan-el-Khalili bazaar and are about to cross at right angles the prolongation of the Muski street by which we approached it, noticing on our right before the crossing the Turkish mosque of Sheik Moutahhar. Beyond the crossing on the right the fifteenth-century mosque of Achraf-Barsbai intervenes before the next crossing of the street of El-

Azhar. Immediately beyond we see one of the most charming views in the old city, produced by the buildings of the Sultan El-Ghouri on each side of the narrow street. We are now in the last phase of the Mamelukes, for these buildings are of sixteenth-century date. His madrasa on the right makes a splendid effect with its lofty façade and three-stage minaret; his mausoleum on the left has a fine matching entrance portal; both of the interiors should be visited. Diverge slightly towards the left in order to see, behind the mausoleum, El-Ghouri's third building, a splendid caravanserai now adapted as a technical school.

We have now seen the best of the Kasaba. Further on, on the right, is the large mosque of Mamluk-al-Muayyad dating from 1415 AD whose bronze entrance doors were purloined from the mosque of Sultan Hasan. There is an enormous courtyard but nothing else remarkable We are now at the southern gate, Bab-Zoueila, and the end of the Fatimid city. The gate is not less impressive than its northern counterparts. It has a sinister place in Cairo history; it was beneath its portal that was crucified the last of the independent Mameluke sultans after the Turkish conquest of 1517 AD.

From the Bab-el-Zoueila one may turn westward and arrive in half a mile at the western boundary of the Fatimid city and a square called Ahmed Maher. Here we find the second of the great Cairo museums of historic Egypt, the Islamic Museum. This is on the scale of the Coptic Museum and really owes its existence to the same sad reason, the decay and neglect of the historic buildings of Cairo. The Museum possesses some fine collections of Islamic objects, notably the Harari collection of bronzes once in the Victoria and Albert Museum. But to a large extent its foundation was inspired by the desire to house objects from local excavations and to rescue furnishings and decorative details from the city's famous buildings. Many of the smaller items, notably ivories and ceramics, derive from recent excavations upon the site of Fostat. From the mosques of Cairo comes the important and unique collection of hanging lamps made it is thought in Syria. Larger relics, notably doors, mihrabs and wooden panels, are abundant; in many cases their provenance is known, so that if the memory is sufficiently keen and accurate they can mentally be fitted into the mosques or other buildings from which they came. And inevitably there are the carpets and the tapestries. The Islamic Museum may not be the greatest of the world's museums but it has performed a vital service in preserving for posterity the objects which once gave life to so many of the great buildings of mediaeval Cairo. A main street takes us back to the Tahrir Square where we see confronting us still the greatest of all Cairene museums, the museum of Ancient Egypt.

7   ANCIENT EGYPT

Much of Ancient Egypt may be seen without ever setting foot in the country. The progress and the scale of the excavations combined with the extraordinary proliferation of the objects, large and small, created by the Ancient Egyptians over an enormous period of time, have had the effect that their works are now scattered over all the civilised world. In France there is the famous collection in the Louvre. Italy has considerable collections in the Vatican Museum and at Turin. The Berlin Collection was famous and there are objects on view at Leiden in Holland and at Athens. In the New World there is a formidable exhibition in the Metropolitan Museum of Art in New York and in the museum in Brooklyn. In Britain the British Museum is famous and there are Egyptian objects in the Soane Museum in London. In Edinburgh the Royal Scottish Museum has a selection. At Oxford and Cambridge the Asmolean and Fitzwilliam Museums are both rich in Egyptian antiquities, as are the University Museums at Liverpool and at Durham. And the Birmingham City Museum and Art Gallery is well provided in this respect.

Of all these collections the most famous are the Louvre and the British Museum, the reason for their pre-eminence being that it was the French and the British who were able to get in first on the long-drawn-out business of removing Egypt's treasures. In the Louvre the larger objects are on the ground floor on the south and east sides of the courtyard. Colossal statues, steles, granite columns, carved sandstone groups, bas-reliefs, sarcophagi, sphinxes, canopic jars proliferate; a special treasure is the carved seated figure of the scribe known as the 'Scribe Accroupi' and dating from the Old Kingdom. The smaller objects are upstairs on the south side of the courtyard, where eight halls or rooms take us chronologically from the prehistoric to the Ptolemaic period; it is worth making a longer pause than usual in the fifth room where the Amarna collection is displayed.

The British Museum collection is similarly divided; larger objects on the ground floor, smaller objects upstairs and the Museum confesses to owning over 70,000 separate objects including, as it claims, the world's greatest collection of the papyri of Ancient Egypt. In terms of Egyptology its greatest prize is certainly the Rosetta stone which confronts the visitor almost immediately on the ground floor; this, as we have seen, is the stone dating from Ptolemaic times which by recording a decree in three languages side by side provided the clue to the Ancient Egyptian hieroglyphics. This early confrontation is due to the fact that the ground floor exhibits are arranged so to speak in reverse, the Greek period coming first and the exhibits leading chronologically backwards into pre-history. A striking object is the sarcophagus of Nectanebis II, said to have been the last native Egyptian ruler before Alexander's conquest. When we get to the New Kingdom, Rameses II inevitably obtrudes; his most striking monument here is the colossal bust in granite successfully abstracted by Belzoni from his mortuary temple at Thebes and long known for some reason as the Young Memnon. Noticeable also is the carved scarab, one of the stranger obsessions of the ancient Egyptians; the scarab beetle was identified with the god Khepri and this example is claimed to be the largest known. A number of Pharaohs of the great period are on view, notably Amenophis III, but the remainder of the sculpture gallery is perhaps more attractive and interesting by reason of its sculptures of non-royal persons; there is an attractive funerary statue of a noble and his wife dating from the Eighteenth Dynasty and a curious block statue of the same period of Sennefer, treasurer of Tuthmosis III. The Middle Kingdom is well represented by statues of Sesostris III; the Old Kingdom by interesting reliefs of scenes of daily life taken from mastaba tombs.

Upstairs two of the rooms are devoted to coffins and mummies, not omitting mummies of animals, fish and birds. In the third room we encounter some of the vast collection of papyri, also some excellent scenes of tomb paintings of Egyptian daily life. There follows the enormous display of smaller objects, statuettes, wood carvings, ivories, models, glass, pottery, jewellery, coins. Collections on this scale are not easily absorbed and one can only be selective; justifiably famous is a funerary statuette of Katep and Hetepheres, a crudely attractive work of the Old Kingdom; among the glass and pottery it is worth while searching, here as everywhere, for examples from the period of Amarna. The visitor to the British Museum collection, however much he may be obsessed with Ancient Egypt, should not ignore the later collection appropriately housed in the Coptic Corridor.

And so to the Museum of Ancient Egypt in Cairo. This Museum, as already noticed, was only established after a long-drawn-out battle, a battle to persuade the nineteenth-century rulers of Egypt to take some effective interest in their own national heritage. The first hero of the battle was the French scholar and archaeologist Mariette and it is certainly appropriate that his marble tomb and bronze statue should now be located in the museum garden. Mariette succeeded in founding the museum in 1857 (long after the Louvre and the British Museum had already built up considerable collections.) Located first at Bulak, it was removed to a discarded palace of Ismail; then at the turn of the century a more responsible attitude supervened and the present imposing building was put up on the north side of what is now Tahrir Square. In the twentieth century there has also been a great change in the official attitude concerning excavations and discoveries. From being a free-for-all country, Egypt has become belatedly jealous of its heritage and considerable precautions are now in force to prevent objects of interest leaving the country. The consequence has been an enormous increase in the number of objects to be guarded in Egypt itself. Alexandria, as we have seen, has its own museum and we shall also see a small and excellent museum at Luxor; but overwhelmingly the treasures of Ancient Egypt now pour into the Cairo Museum. Already there are over 100,000 objects on display in addition to considerable reserves hidden away in stores or basements.

This constant inflow necessitates periodical re-arrangements so that no description of the museum can hope long to be up-to-date. But in the main respect the museum follows the example of the Louvre and the British Museum in having its larger objects on the ground floor and its smaller objects upstairs. In the upstairs room a sensible attempt has been made to organise some of the exhibits by categories such as mummies, jewellery and coins, but otherwise the arrangement attempts to be chronological and on both floors by doing the museum clockwise one can follow Ancient Egypt on its historical course. Downstairs the first nine halls are devoted to the Old Kingdom. The most famous items here are probably the seated figure, carved in diorite, of Chephren builder of the Second Pyramid of Giza and found there in his valley temple; and the wooden carving from Sakkara known as the Village Headman from its supposed resemblance to numerous modern examples of that functionary. One can hardly fail also to be struck by the colouring which still survives on the limestone statue of Prince Ra-hotep and his wife Nofret found in his tomb at Meidum.

The four halls following cover the Middle Kingdom and the Intermediate Period. Sesostris I, the Great Pharaoh of the Twelfth Dynasty, is here commemorated by ten over-life-size statues from his mortuary temple in his pyramid at Lisht; Mentonhotep of the previous dynasty by a crude but effective statue in sandstone still bearing some of its colour decoration.

We now come to the New Empire, the most prolific period of Ancient Egypt. An effective grouping in one of the halls brings together some of the best sculpture of the Eighteenth Dynasty, featuring notably Tuthmosis III and his successors Amenophis II and III; an entertaining moment is the rotund figure of the Queen of Punt with her thin husband beside her. Then a welcome interlude is provided by a complete hall sensibly devoted to the Amarna period and the strange religion of Akhenaten including his own magnificent head in limestone; after which we begin to notice appearances of Tutankhamen. In time we reach the Nineteenth Dynasty with the inevitable Rameses II. The largest objects are to be found in the so called Central Atrium, including a colossal group of Amenophis III and his wife Teye. To see the later period it is necessary to move round to the eastern galleries, displaying in chronological order the Ethiopian and Persian epochs, followed by the Ptolemies, the Romans and the Copts. Some of the grandest relics of these periods are to be seen in the so-called Great Gallery of Honour which completes one's clockwise journey back to the main entrance.

On the first floor one may make a similar progression. Striking survivals from the Middle Kingdom are the groups of figures set in the scenes of their daily lives, most notably the groups of soldiers found in the tomb of a general called Mesah in the province of Assiout. In subsequent halls are astonishing displays of ancient models of the utensils and properties used by the Ancient Egyptians, notably their boats with all their apparatus; and then the incredible outpourings of furnishings provided in the tombs of the notables, the prelude to Tutankhamen. Before seeing Tutankhamen it is possible to view the royal mummies, a macabre spectacle, and the coffins of every epoch, or more cheerfully the room of the coins and the room of the jewellery.

Tutankhamen at the time of writing occupies the whole of the northern and eastern galleries. It is an astonishing commentary on the Ancient Egyptians, as well as on those generations who have subsequently plundered their tombs, that he should occupy such an enormous proportion of the space of the modern museum.

His comparatively small tomb clearly was full to bursting; it provokes the morbid question as to the fate of all the centuries of tomb furniture of his much more important predecessors and successors. Possibly after one's first glimpse of the scale of this immense display one's reaction may be to offer thanks that the contents of most of the other royal tombs of Egypt have in fact perished. The unique discovery of his tomb with its enormous contents posed difficult problems of security and taste; they were solved by leaving in position the sarcophagus and the wooden coffin containing the royal mummy; while the inner wooden coffin and the gold coffin in which the mummy was found, together with almost all the other moveable contents of the tomb were taken to Cairo. The gold coffin, a work of unparalleled splendour and sumptuousness, is undoubtedly the show-piece of the display; as to the display as a whole, one can only be astounded at the scale and detail of the furnishings with which it was thought necessary that an Egyptian monarch should be accompanied into the nether world.

Notwithstanding the extraordinary profusion of Ancient Egypt as displayed in the museums and in the excavated sites one must accept that what has survived is concerned not with the lives of the Egyptians but with their deaths. Tomb-chambers, mastabas, pyramids are all different types of memorial to the dead and the innumerable objects on display in the museums are almost without exception articles which, resembling as they obviously do the articles used by the Egyptians in their daily lives, owe their survival to being secreted away in tombs for the use of the dead. The great houses, the royal palaces and their contents have vanished almost without trace; almost all excavation, almost all Egyptian archaeology, is centred round tombs and round the Egyptian obsession with death.

After viewing the museums, and before seeing the ancient sites, it may be useful to try to form some mental picture of this civilisation and to surmise how it all happened. Obviously everything centred round religion and it was round religion that was built up the elaborate tradition that circumscribed everything to do with death.

The religion of the Ancient Egyptians has often been described and it is not a topic which lends itself easily to summary. But an attempt may be made to indicate some of the salient influences and features and to form some picture as to how it grew up. The first thing to accept is that the religion varied greatly through the centuries. The second is that, unlike Christianity and Mahommedanism, it was never monotheistic. The third is that it was in a high degree local. The earliest picture of Egyptian religion is of local gods attached to particular areas or towns and probably unrecognised elsewhere. We must assume that as places grew in importance, so their gods grew with them. The result was an astonishing proliferation of gods. Another result was the periodical transformation of their positions and importance. The gods developed the legends of their own histories, often branching out into family relationships; when civilisation expanded and gods came into contact with each other, they were often identified and sometimes amalgamated. To recount the full history of Egyptian religion one would have to tell it first in terms of time and secondly in terms of place and then the story would be incomplete.

There was an enormous identification of gods with objects, with good and evil features, with plants and above all with animals. The sun and moon were obvious objects of worship, but more earthly objects are heard of, stones, posts, columns. Love and joy, peace and war, fertility and prosperity, were obvious attributes to be fastened on to individual gods. Trees and plants were favourite objects for identification. Above all was the obsession with animals; cows, bulls, rams, goats, crocodiles, cats, lions, frogs, fishes, ibises, falcons and vultures were all believed at one time or other to be chosen by gods as their abode and as the forms in which they desired to be recognised and worshipped. These facts go far to explain the extraordinary representations of their gods in which the Egyptians specialised. Among those with which we shall become most familiar are gods in human form but with heads and faces of birds and animals, gods carrying cows' horns on their heads, gods surmounted by a serpent, gods standing, gods seated, gods struck in some traditional posture, gods carrying every variety of stave. All this works in very well with the hieroglyphics, long the major mystery of Ancient Egypt.

The most popular and persistent religious story of Ancient Egypt was probably that of Osiris, the god of vegetation and fertility. Egypt under the rule of Osiris was enjoying peace and prosperity when his wicked brother Seth conspired against him and forced him into a chest which was then closed and thrown into the Nile. The chest travelled down the Nile and across the sea to Phoenicia. It was eventually discovered by his wife Isis who took it back to Egypt and buried it before going to visit her son Horus in the Delta. During her absence Seth found the body, cut it into fourteen

pieces and scattered the fragments. As soon as Isis discovered this,
she sought out the fragments and wherever she discovered one
erected a suitable monument. When Horus grew up he set out to
avenge the murder and was eventually victorious, and finished
up by magically restoring his father to life and Osiris thereafter
ruled the land as king of the dead. His principal burial place was
regarded as being at Abydos where his head was buried; and Abydos
became from the time of the Fifth Dynasty the object of a cult of
quite incredible intensity.

Notwithstanding the fame of Osiris, the most considerable god
throughout Egyptian history was probably Re, the god of the Sun.
Re appears in many contexts and as religious fashions rose and
fell it was his fate to be amalgamated with a variety of other gods.
A more congenial goddess, who will often be encountered in Upper
Egypt, is Hathor, the goddess of love and joy. Her particular home
was Dendera and she was for some reason always portrayed with
cow's horns on her head. Horus, who played such a distinguished
part in the story of Osiris, became recognised as the royal god and
as the patron of the Pharaohs and god of the empire; he is portrayed
usually with a falcon's head. Ptah, originally a local god of Memphis,
later acquired a wider fame; portrayed as a very correct gentleman
with a beard and in a standing posture, he is shown as carrying a
complicated stave and was revered as the patron of artists. He had
a rather alarming wife Sekhmet portrayed usually with a lion's
head bearing an orb: on the one hand she was the destroyer of
mankind, on the other she was the goddess of healing. Among the
strangest looking gods was Thoth, portrayed usually with the head
of an ibis and generally regarded as the moon-god, responsible
for wisdom, intellect and learning. Almost equally strange was
Anubis portrayed with the head of a jackal and responsible particularly for the dead and with everything to do with embalming.

Three gods who make an exceptional impact on the visitor are
Apis, Aten and Amun. Apis was the god who was considered to be
enshrined in the sacred bulls of Memphis. As each sacred bull
died, the priests of Memphis had first to organise his ceremonial
burial and then to identify the new bull which Apis had made his
emblem. It is this weird cult which was responsible for the astonishing serapeum or bull cemetery which we shall see at Sakkara. Aten
was the god of the sun-disk and is habitually portrayed as such with
rays radiating from the disk and ending in hands. From compara-
tive obscurity he was elevated to primacy among the gods by the
determination and fanatical zeal of the Pharaoh Amenophis IV

who built for him the special capital of Amarna and in his honour changed his own name to Akhenaten. This was but a short-lived interlude in the long supremacy of Amun. Amun was originally an unimportant local god of Thebes. With the establishment of the New Kingdom and the great expansion of Luxor and Karnak and the City of the Dead on the western bank the power and fame of Amun increased also; he was identified with the almighty Re and as Amun-Re for many centuries he dominated the Egyptian religious world. The scale of his cult and the power of the organisation which supported it can be dimly appreciated when we view the gigantic temples erected in his honour.

The gods were obviously involved in the issue which clearly dominated Egyptian religious thought, the issue of the future life. As religious theory developed this became particularly the domain of Osiris and the story of his death and re-birth became the model of what was in store for mortals after death. The conviction that the life of man continued after death was responsible for the three customs which have caused such extensive relics to be preserved through the centuries. First, the body had to be safeguarded. Grisly details have been recorded by Herodotus and others as to how the corpse was treated after death; certain parts of the body were extracted to be preserved in the so-called canopic jars while for the body itself the process of embalming became widespread if not universal. Hence the extraordinary number of mummies, carefully preserved and elaborately wrapped in linen, which have survived to modern times. Secondly, suitable residences had to be provided for the deceased. The size of these depended on the wealth and resources of the family and those which have survived range from the humblest little tombs to the Great Pyramid. Most familiar of the survivals are those on the scale of large or small houses, usually excavated or built beneath ground level, which have been found all over Egypt. Great importance was clearly attached to their decoration, thanks to which posterity has been given an astonishing insight into the manners and customs of this ancient world. Thirdly, the deceased had to be provided with all the utensils and provisions which he would need to sustain him in the next world. Objects often of great value were enclosed in the tomb and their variety and comprehensiveness is astonishing. Also enormous efforts were made to hide and safeguard them for eternity. This was the origin of that most astonishing of all burial initiatives, the Valley of the Kings at Thebes. Notwithstanding all efforts and precautions, these treasures became through the centuries the prey of tomb-robbers and what has survived is due to the haphazard play of chance. The discovery of Tutankhamen's tomb with its amazing contents gives some idea of the original scale of the custom and of the quantity and value of what has been lost.

Since much of what the visitor sees relates to individual Pharaohs the question arises as to how the Egyptian rulers fitted into this complicated religious setting. In spite of the power which some of them wielded, the evidence does not suggest that they themselves were worshipped as gods. As we have seen in tracing their history, they were in no way immune from the customary vicissitudes of royal dynasties; intrigues and passions, family relationships and family jealousies, wars and battles played their inevitable part; at many moments of their history Pharaohs must have appeared as anything but super-human. We are in the realm of surmise but it seems a fair surmise that the most successful Pharaohs were those who established a royal establishment in league with a priestly establishment without permitting the priestly establishment to boss the show. It is difficult to believe that enterprises like the Great Pyramid could have been fastened onto the Egyptian people except as part of a passionate belief that they were fulfilling a sacred duty. The building of the gigantic temples is more easily under-standable; much as they exceed in size any comparable constructions in other countries or other ages, they are but expressions of that urge, which at times seems to take possession of all civilisations, that visible expression must be given to the glory of their gods. Some of the Pharaohs clearly played a major part in these enterprises but their part was probably on the one hand to provide the resources and on the other to receive much of the glorification. Hence the colossal statues of Rameses II and others which make such astonish-ing contributions to the temple scenes. To all these surmises one qualification must be made. There were clearly occasions in Egyptian history when religion and the gods were called in aid to justify the accession of a new ruler and this sometimes went as far as providing him with a godly ancestry.

An enormous commentary on all this has been recorded for posterity in papyri and hieroglyphics. Papyri are a matter for the museum and the specialist but one can hardly enter a tomb or a temple without encountering the hieroglyphics. These are the inscriptions, sometimes painted, sometimes incised, sometimes carved in raised relief, which cover objects such as sarcophagi, the pillars and columns which support the tombs and temples, and the walls and surfaces of the tombs and temples themselves. The proliferation is astounding; in some of the largest temples one is left with the feeling that it was a point of honour that not a square foot should be left uncovered. The deciphering and reading of all these is obviously a matter for an expert. For the amateur who wants to have a try perhaps the best way is to start on the so-called cartouches of the individual Pharaohs. These are cylindrical frames, rounded at top and bottom and taller than they are wide, containing a number of apparently meaningless symbols and diagrams. Thus Cheops, builder of the Great Pyramid, has in the lower half of his cartouche what appears to be a small chicken with, above it, a similar small chicken gazing at a round ball. In the later dynasties the cartouches are more elaborate and generally dual; by the time of Rameses II there are at least a dozen figures within the two cylinders and Tutankhamen, unimportant though he was, has even more.

But it is time to see Ancient Egypt, so to speak, on the ground. In the Delta, as we have already noticed, it has virtually disappeared. The greater part which survives is spread along the Nile journey into Upper Egypt. But round Cairo are some of the most sensational relics and these can be visited by car in a series of single days. Let us start then with a modest trip, taking us not further than the city suburbs, and then launch out further upon the great monuments of the Old Kingdom.

Seven miles north-east of Cairo was the ancient city of Heliopolis, famous as the centre of the worship of the Sun-god. Heliopolis is now but a suburban prolongation of Cairo, but in ancient times, though it was apparently never a national capital, it came next to Karnak in the hierarchy of priestly strongholds and its temple was famous. Today only one considerable relic of its ancient greatness survives, an obelisk: a not unsuitable survival, for Heliopolis appears to have been the original and principal projector of this peculiarly Egyptian form of monument.

Striking in themselves and easily transportable, obelisks became objects of plunder of successive conquerors; the Romans in particular appreciated them and modern countries have followed their example. The greatest of all obelisks stands near the basilica of St John Lateran in Rome, a famous example stands in front of St Peter's, and there are said still to be ten others in the city, while one was removed to Constantinople. A Roman ruler moved two from Heliopolis to Alexandria; by Mehemet Ali these were presented one to Great Britain, one to the United States; one now adorns Central Park in New York, the other stands as Cleopatra's

Needle on the Victoria Embankment in London. A famous example had been presented earlier to King Louis Philippe of France who had it set up in the centre of the Place de la Concorde; another, more strangely, found its way to the garden of Kingston Lacy in Dorset. Only five or six are still to be found in Egypt, some at Karnak; the interest of the surviving example at Heliopolis, erected nearly two thousand years before Christ, is that it is the earliest known example of the species.

But from Cairo the great excursions to Ancient Egypt are to the Pyramids. A journey of only seven or eight miles from the city centre takes one through the suburbs and the intensely cultivated zone and then—so sudden are the transitions of Egypt—onto the desert plateau which forms the Pyramid platform. Vaguely one registers the nineteenth-century accompaniment of the Pyramids, the Mena House Hotel. Then the Great Pyramid, visible almost from the start of the journey and minute by minute increasing in scale, presents itself in all its immensity.

The statistics, for those who like statistics, are impressive. The Great Pyramid is a perfect square, each side 746 feet in length. The present height, somewhat less than the original, is 450 feet (St Paul's Cathedral 365 feet). The cubic content of the masonry is more than 3,000,000 cubic yards. The Pyramid covers an area of nearly 13 acres.

More interesting, though more speculative, are the statistics concerned with the actual building. The method of building, considering the perennial skill of the Egyptians in making earth roads, is not difficult to imagine. What boggles the imagination is how, in a time when modern engineering was unknown, the human resources were mobilised to achieve a construction of these dimensions.

The project depended obviously upon the seasons of the Nile; upon the fact that during certain months of the year the Egyptian peasant was debarred from any profitable agricultural activity. Based upon this must have been a conscription of labour upon an unprecedented scale. Herodotus, the oldest of our historians, states that some 100,000 men were employed annually for three months. They first made the road for the transport of the stones from the Nile to the Pyramid plateau and this took ten years. They then spent another twenty years building the Pyramid itself. The Pyramid gives the impression of being a single original design, but modern experts cast their doubts on this. The Pyramid, they think, was designed originally as a much smaller building; was then, as Cheops' reign continued, enlarged; and was then enlarged again to make its present size.

The Pyramid can be both entered and ascended. Infinite trouble to conceal the entrance was taken by the ancient Egyptians. The Pyramid was entered nevertheless in ancient times; it was restored and entered again by the Persians, by the Romans, by the Arabs. A number of European travellers achieved entry in the eighteenth century. In recent times more serious and responsible investigations have been made and more statistics have been established. The Pyramid is now open to the tourist. It is not an expedition which one can unguardedly recommend. In the words of the immortal Baedeker, it should be omitted by nervous or delicate persons, especially those predisposed to apoplectic or fainting fits. The interior of the Pyramid is in fact airless, dark and claustrophobic. A long succession of passages takes one into the Great Hall. Beyond the Great Hall one may reach the King's Chamber containing an empty and damaged sarcophagus which, it is believed, once contained the body of Cheops.

The ascent of the Pyramid is an expedition of a very different kind. No airlessness or claustrophobia here; the only enemy is *le vertige*. A couple or group of Beduin is on hand to assist the traveller, who has nothing to lose except his dignity. By pulling and, above all, pushing, the traveller is raised from step to step; and when he pauses for breath, the contemplation of the steps is not uninteresting. The Pyramid, or its outer casing, is built of huge blocks of stone of equal height (about three feet). The climb has been made possible by mediaeval Arabs who, in order to build Cairo, levered out the casing stones which originally made the Pyramid an unclimable glacis. The original visual effect may be judged by looking at the topmost reaches of the Second Pyramid where the covering still remains and which is thus a climb only for the expert mountaineer. On the top of the Great Pyramid a sizeable platform has been formed; from it, it is said, King Edward VIII when Prince of Wales drove a golf ball into the desert. It is the desert in fact which makes the greatest impression in the view. The rest is detail: the distant Cairo with its Citadel and minarets; the Nile; the suburbs and the road by which we have come; distant, remoter, pyramids; the occasional palm groves; then nearer to us the Sphinx, the Third Pyramid, the Second Pyramid and the minute but complicated relics of the ancient burial ground at our feet.

For the Pyramid was by no means self-contained. To the west of it extends a vast cemetery of the Kings, regularly laid out, in which large numbers of contemporary officials and dignitaries had their last resting place. Little now remains, on the East side, of the Mortuary Temple which was the essential accompaniment of every Pyramid and in which the deceased Pharaoh could be worshipped. But relics do survive nearby of three small Pyramids built in honour of members of the Royal Family; the middle one, according to Herodotus, the tomb of Cheops' daughter; the most southerly one, according to an inscription in the Cairo museum, the tomb of his Queen. And not far from them the relics of a number of mastabas commemorating sons and daughters of the Royal House. A more striking discovery made in recent times on the south side of the Pyramid has been the splendid ship made of cedar of Lebanon destined to ferry the King in the company of the sun into the next world.

The Mortuary Temples are better appreciated at the Second and Third Pyramids. That at the Third Pyramid (the Pyramid of Mykerinos) is said to have been virtually complete as recently as 1755 AD. In both cases the Temples are now a mass of ruins but their dimensions can easily be absorbed. From each of them ancient causeways, recognisable in part, lead downwards to the fourth great object in this complex, the Sphinx.

The Sphinx was not built; it was excavated. More statistics are here in place: the Sphinx is 240 feet long, 66 feet high; its ear 4½ feet, its nose 5½ feet and its mouth 7½ feet. Sadly, the Sphinx through the ages has been mutilated and it is unkind to examine it in detail; at a distance its majesty remains. The inspiration has been attributed to Chephren, builder of the Second Pyramid who, quarrying for building stone on the site, struck a knoll of unsuitable limestone and decreed the shaping of it into a Sphinx, making the Sphinx the guardian of the sacred enclosure of his Pyramid. Close to it is Chephren's temple known as the Valley Temple, a structure which in any other surroundings would merit a special visit of its own. The dimensions of the temple are in fact given as being 147 feet square and 43 feet in height. Originally entered by large portals on the east side, the temple has now to be approached from the inclined corridor which led to the Pyramid. The central feature is a large hypostyle hall containing sixteen monolithic granite columns; on each side are storerooms. On the site is the shaft in which was found the splendid personal memorial of Chephren: the great diorite statue now in the Cairo Museum.

The Pyramids we have seen — generally called 'The Pyramids' — are at Giza. Neither Giza nor Cairo itself were ancient sites but the choice of location must have been dictated by Memphis, the splendid capital of all Egypt during the Old Kingdom and some later ages. Memphis no longer exists but its site has been identified some seven miles south west of Cairo and on the west bank of the Nile. The Pyramids we have seen, though by far the most famous, form but a small proportion in the catalogue of Ancient Egyptian tomb sites; at least seventy-two pyramids have been identified. A high proportion of them stretched in a north-south line along the fringe of the desert on the west side of the Nile. From North to South the first were at Abu Rawash where there is little left to see; it was said in 1881 that stone was being carried away at the rate of 300 camel-loads a day. Next comes Giza.

South of Giza are Abusir and Sakkara. Abusir has four surviving pyramids, all in poor condition, with relics of funeral temples and mastabas. Sakkara, further south, is the greatest funeral site of Ancient Egypt. While the Pyramids of Giza are of the Fourth Dynasty, the famous Step-Pyramid of Sakkara is known to have been built by Zoser, a Pharaoh of the Third. But before admiring the Pyramid we must pause for a construction of a later age and visit the Bulls. These were the Sacred Bulls of Apis buried in the Serapeum, one of the more grotesque creations of Ancient Egypt. One plunges underground into a great corridor where, regularly ranged against the wall are gigantic sarcophagi each about eleven feet high, containing the relics of these monsters. It is hard to believe that this ritual carried on through the Persian conquest and into the time of the Ptolemies; perhaps the most fascinating moment is the last tomb, already in the corridor but abandoned before being levered into its proper resting-place.

Between the Serapeum and the Pyramid is the house of Mariette, the famous French archaeologist to whom, more than any other modern figure, the preservation of the treasures of Ancient Egypt is due. And near Mariette's house is the tomb of Ti.

The tomb of Ti is one of the most engaging of Egyptian experiences. Ti was an important official and landowner of the Fifth Dynasty: he is shown in the entrance vestibule in wig and apron holding in one hand a staff and in the other a kind of club. The tomb, which is as large as a house, with rooms and corridors, is elaborately adorned with mural reliefs, many excellently preserved. They bring to life, as nowhere else in Egypt, this ancient civilisation, in some ways not so different from our own. Here we see ploughing and sowing, rams treading in the seed, cattle being driven, fish being caught; we see ship-building and carpentering; we see Ti magisterially steering his boat through the tall reeds of the marshes and Ti in his estate office busy with the records and accounts.

For those whose taste is whetted there are other comparable tombs nearby. In the tomb of Ptahhotep the emphasis is all on physical effort and outdoor effects; we see running and wrestling; we see lions and gazelles and hares and hedgehogs. Then the care, once again, of cattle; the processes of wine-making; and then once more the hunt, sometimes in the marshes and sometimes in the desert. So again in the tomb of Mereruka, though here the artist has permitted himself more extravagances; goldsmiths are seen busy making necklaces and vessels; a lion is devouring a bull; hippopotami are being speared while a hippopotamus takes the floor with a crocodile in its mouth. As one emerges from such visions one becomes aware that one is in a huge area of tombs, some in actual streets; how many more visions are waiting to be revealed is impossible to say.

But we have diverged from the Step-Pyramid. The unique interest of this pyramid is, that as far as human records can tell us, this was the first building ever built of stone. Incredibly, across five thousand years, it has a human and a personal story. It was a personal servant of the Pharaoh, a grand vizier who was also an expert architect, who persuaded the Pharaoh of the practicality of the scheme. If the Pyramid is called after Zoser, the credit is due to Imhotep. Clearly they were taking no chances. Though the general form of a pyramid is maintained, they did not attempt the smooth glacis effect of the pyramids of Giza. The Step-Pyramid was, we are assured, sheeted with smooth stone like its successors, but the building was graded in stages, a series of decreasing rectangles — for this pyramid is not square — each stage superimposed on the lower course. Not to be ignored on this visit is the Pyramid of Unas, the last Pharaoh of the Fifth Dynasty, which can be both climbed and entered; the Pharaoh's granite sarcophagus survives in the tomb-chamber. Close to this pyramid are three shaft tombs thought to be of the Persian period involving vertical excavations in the rock more than sixty feet in depth. One detail of Sakkara revealing the incredible profusion of Ancient Egypt is the fact that in the Step Pyramid no less than 30,000 earthenware vessels have been found.

From the Step-Pyramid one can diverge to the actual site of Memphis. This is an enormous area, now mostly planted as a palm grove, silent witness of the great capital which during so many centuries Memphis was. Endless heaps of earth and rubble cover the site. For the seeker after sights little enough remains. Two colossal statues of Rameses II were found; one now transported to the main station square of Cairo; the other presented by Mehemet Ali in 1820 to the British Museum but never removed and now housed on the site under a modern shed. Not far off is the alabaster Sphinx, thought to date from the Nineteenth Dynasty and to weigh about eighty tons. No city of Ancient Egypt had a longer or more distinguished history. Essentially linked with the worship of the god Ptah, the city dated, it is thought, from the time of the first Pharaoh Menes and did not finally decline until the foundations (at a thousand years interval) of Alexandria and Cairo; and its ruins are recorded as being still impressive in mediaeval times.

But we have by no means exhausted the sequence of the pyramids. South of the Step-Pyramid are a further series of Sakkara pyramids, of the Fifth and Sixth Dynasties and further south still are the pyramids of Dahshur. The latter are of various dates; the most interesting is the great stone pyramid of Snefru, the predecessor of Cheops, for though not so large as the Great Pyramid of Cheops, and not so ancient as the Step-Pyramid, it is the oldest of all the true pyramids. A curiosity not far off is the so-called 'Blunted Pyramid.' Some miles to the south, at Meidum, is another pyramid of Snefru, in some ways the most appealing of all the Pyramids for its is the most mysterious. As seen now it has the appearance of a pyramid built on a gigantic heap of rubble which gives the whole structure an illusion of enormous height. The pyramid has been entered and a tomb-chamber has been found but no sarcophagus. It is a pyramid of eternal unanswered questions: was it ever a true burial place for its founder? how has the structure come to be resting on its present enormous but apparently unstable mass?

Meidum lies close to the Faiyum, one of the greater geographical curiosities of Egypt. A vast area of depression, carved as it were out of the edge of the Western Desert and containing still the large fresh-water Lake Karoun, it is rendered intensely fertile by a canal from the Nile which, whether or not attributable to human ingenuity, has from time immemorial brought intense agricultural prosperity to the area. The Faiyum is now really an excursion from Cairo for the tourist with time on his hands; replete with historical interest, it preserves, like Memphis, only a few scanty relics of its ancient fame. From the mainline station of Beni Suef in the Nile Valley it is a few miles to the site of Heracleopolis and further north to the modern town of Lahoun which marks the entrance to the Faiyum.

The principal town, Medinet-el-Faiyum, is on or near the site of the strangely named Crocodilopolis so called, as its name implies, from being the centre of the worship of the sacred crocodiles. On our way to this site we have passed the site of the ancient Labyrinth. Credulity in Egypt is so frequently put to the test that the stranger becomes capable of believing almost anything, but it is still hard to believe the accounts of ancient writers about the Labyrinth. Herodotus, Strabo, Pliny, who had seen the Great Pyramid, who had seen the Sphinx, are all agreed that the Labyrinth was the most wonderful building of Egypt, a gigantic assemblage of palaces and temples; its courts, said Strabo, were entered by long covered passages, 'intersecting each other and thus forming such a winding path that a stranger cannot find his way into or out of each court without a guide.' Of all this nothing now remains but the familiar heaps of earth and rubble. What remains in or near the Faiyum are the pyramid of Lahoun; the pyramid of Hawara; and a number of sepulchral chambers which rank with the most remarkable in Egypt.

We have now made a fairly long progression for the Faiyum is some sixty miles south of Cairo. But at Meidum which is close to the Faiyum we have reached the end of the pyramids and of the major monuments of the Old Kingdom. In all this progression, except when we have entered the Faiyum, we have never been far from the Nile and the tourist who prefers the river steamer can in fact make some of the pyramid visits from a Nile base. But from now on the advantage is all with the river boat and against the car. The great journey up the river lies ahead of us. It is necessary to return in spirit to Cairo and embark.

8   FROM CAIRO TO LUXOR

There cannot be any experience in the world that much resembles a boat trip up the Nile. Other rivers have their boats and their navigation, some have distinguished cities and buildings on their banks, some have much more sensational natural scenery; but none can combine the feeling of mystery and antiquity that is the characteristic of the Nile. The modern towns may not differ much from what may be seen elsewhere in the Arab world; but the tombs and the temples are something apart, mute witnesses of the astonishing achievement of this incredibly ancient world.

The counterpart to all this antiquity is the intense modern life that goes on along the banks. So narrow is the cultivated valley strip, so intensive is the agriculture, that one is seldom out of sight of a village and as often as not one is in sight of the human population. It is a world which the modern Nile traveller perforce sees mostly at a distance; then the boat draws into the bank to make a call at some ancient site and the landing-place is immediately surrounded; mostly by eager faced children enthusiastically demanding bakshish. Sadly there is seldom opportunity to visit the villages themselves, but at a distance their two landmarks are generally visible, the minaret and the pigeon-house, with the addition in Christian areas of the projecting roof or dome of a Coptic church.

One of the pleasurable, if melancholy, ways of killing time on the river journey is reflecting on the lives of the fellahin. As one watches the laborious processes of cultivation, often carried on in the most primitive fashion, it is extraordinary to think what this has supported through the ages; hundreds of Pharaohs, probably hundreds of thousands of priests, the construction and expense of dozens of pyramids, temples, cities, palaces and tens of thousands of elaborate tombs; the Persians, the Greeks and the Romans; the Christian monks and all the Coptic establishment; then the Moslem mosques with all that goes with them; the splendours of the Caliphs and the extortions and depredations of the Mamelukes; the follies and fantastic extravagances of the Khedives and Kings of modern times; the huge burdens of armaments and warlike provision for the recent wars against Israel. Though Egypt has now some industry and though the cotton cultivation has brought a great accession of wealth, the true resources of the country still derive, as they have always done, from the willingness of the fellahin to continue patiently, remorselessly, their annual round of cultivation according to the traditional age-long routine.

Some of the accessories of this astonishing way of life make themselves evident to the traveller. Every now and again is audible the chug-chug which means the mechanical pump now used to raise water from the river level. Away from the river and amidst the network of irrigation channels and canals the older devices are more likely to be met with; the bucket suspended from the long pole with the heavy weight at the other end, or the more elaborate arrangement of interlocking wooden screws which needs a patient animal to activate it and which produces an endless stream of water from the little pots which rotate with the wheel. The favourite animal of the fellahin is the buffalo which, judging by its expression, is a beast of infinite patience and content; the great luxury of the buffalo which makes him frequently visible to the traveller is a bathe or a wallow in the Nile. Curious flocks of sheep are in evidence, with large tails which serve the purpose of water-reservoirs in the same way as do the humps of camels; nearer the villages are the even more curious chickens whose survival is a mystery for they obstinately refuse to hatch their own eggs. Camels themselves are animals of the desert rather than the valley but on the larger farms they perform valuable service as beasts of burden and nothing is stranger than the sight of a camel laden with sugar canes.

The villages, when one does penetrate to them, impress with their invariable characteristic: they are all built of mud. This apparently menial type of construction has by no means been confined to the peasantry; in our visits to some of the grandest temples of antiquity, we shall find that while the temples are built of stone, their surrounding walls, sometimes of enormous scale and size, are entirely built of mud bricks. Possibly only their scale and size has enabled them to survive; nothing is more friable or perishable than a mud brick wall and the simple houses of the fellahin must undergo a constant process of building, collapse and restoration. The biggest question-mark overhanging the whole future of the fellahin and Egyptian agriculture is the question of mechanical cultivation and modern methods.

The connoisseur of wild life should not on his Nile journey ignore the birds. Next to the pigeons which populate every Nile village the most evident birds are probably the egrets who live a happy life not only on the river but also in the marshes and the irrigation canals. The Nile valley has its native birds in some abundance but its primary importance in the bird-world is as a transit route. Enormous annual migrations from north to south and south to north use this obviously attractive way through the African continent. The migrating flocks are not often on view to the Nile passenger, but the specialist will notice with interest the birds which do appear, particularly when, like the kingfisher, they are redolent of one's native land.

Not much will be seen by the traveller of the Nile fish which are said still to populate the river in large numbers and in a great variety of species of which the most famous is the large Nile perch. One native which, unhappily or happily, has been exterminated by modern civilisation is the crocodile, which was still abundant in the nineteenth century but which now is found only in the river's upper reaches well beyond the Egyptian frontier.

Before embarking, a brief word may be said about the physical scenery. This is always the same, but always different. By this paradox is meant that while the unvarying valley framework, the dun-coloured cliffs, are almost always in view, the scene below them varies according to the windings of the river. The valley cliffs are the skyline of the desert, but the desert begins not at their summit but at their feet where the land begins to be above the irrigation level. There are moments when a sudden curve of the river takes one almost to the cliff base; then the river turns and one will be looking across a wide and level agricultural plain before the desert line is reached. Between the river and the cliffs the only intermediate skylines are provided by the villages and the trees. Though fruit trees are seen in the villages, the trees outside are overwhelmingly the picturesque date palms. An astonishing fact about Egypt is that it has not, and never has had, any timber properly so-called. This has always been the most essential import and from the earliest times the Pharaohs took trouble to promote good trading relations with timber-producing countries like the Lebanon.

For those who decide to do Upper Egypt by the river there is no longer much choice of means. Millionaires can still take their private yachts; the ordinary mortal must make the best of the tourist boats let out by the government to the tourist firms.

It was not always thus. The later nineteenth century was certainly one of the most idyllic periods for the Nile voyage. In the winter of 1880 Miss Ellen Hope-Edwardes set out from the depths of Shropshire with her semi-invalid brother; by Christmas-time they were ready to start from Cairo. Their vessel was a dahabieh, a sailing ship of the kind that may still be seen on the Nile today but rather more sumptuously fitted up; in addition to the crew's quarters there were five cabins, for two were needed for the invalid brother and the lady's maid must not be forgotten. The crew amounted to seventeen, consisting of two captains, ten sailors and a cook-boy; this last a little round black creature about nine years old. There were also two cooks and two Maltese waiters, father and son. And of course a dragoman. An outfit of this type cost between £80 and £200 per month and the round trip to Assuan and back would take about four months. There were of course extras to be paid for. Towed behind the dahabieh was a much smaller boat in which chickens and pigeons were to live; before the start of the voyage it was necessary to supply, first, wine for the passengers; secondly, trousers for the crew; and thirdly a drum and tambourine, traditional extras to which all tourists were expected to subscribe. Important extras on the voyage were the sheep which had periodically to be purchased and which, killed and skinned, would be hung on the lower deck; and at the end of the four months' voyage there were the tips to be given, twelve shillings each to the sailors and two pounds each to the captains.

If the modern departure from Cairo is by day, one can happily relive some of one's Cairo experiences. Here as we move past them are the islands of Zamaleh and Roda; there, on each side are the city landmarks, the new tower, the Hilton Hotel, the Citadel; then to the west the Pyramids appear, not only the Great Pyramids of Giza but the chain of pyramids which as we have seen extend south of Sakkara to Meidum. Then the early Egyptian darkness falls and one faces the first night on the Nile voyage.

About 170 miles south of Cairo is Beni Hasan, the base for one of the most interesting excursions into Ancient Egypt. The interest resides principally in the fact that here is a major display of the arts and architecture of that least known period of Ancient Egyptian history, the Middle Kingdom. The Middle Kingdom—following as usual the magisterial Manetho—spread itself through three dynasties, the Eleventh, Twelfth and Thirteenth. Its most brilliant period was the Twelfth Dynasty and this, chiefly, is what we see on this excursion from Beni Hasan.

But there are some preludes. A short way from the river we pass
near the Cat's Grave-yard in which the cats sacred to Pekhet, the
chief goddess of the region, were interred. Pekhet herself is glorified
in a rock-temple built in the time of the New Kingdom by the
joint sovereigns Queen Hatshepsut and King Tuthmosis III. The
latter subsequently erased his sister's name and a later ruler Seti I
inserted his own name in the blanks. Three columns remain and a
number of reliefs.

The Rock-Tombs which are the true object of this excursion are
some half hour's ride from the river side. Thirty-nine in number
and regularly disposed on the rocks, they are not tombs of Pharaohs
or high-priests; though some appear to commemorate members
of princely families, they are essentially memorials of dignitaries
of the town which flourished here in Middle Kingdom times.
Considered simply as structural achievements, they are by no means
to be despised. The method in each case was to drive into the cliff
face for a sufficient distance to supply, first, the interior space
required and, secondly, the necessary thickness of unhewn rock to
provide a roof. Rough pillars would be left for the entrance fronts
while the interior excavation was completed and finally the entrance
fronts would themselves be worked and carved. The view of the
final product of the façades, as seen from the river valley below, is
not the least of the attractions of the site.

But the real interest is of course in the finish and in the decorations
within. The tombs are by no means all on the same plan. The
simplest ones (for example no. 15 and no. 17) consist of a single
room hewn out of the rock ornamented inside with columns but
entered by a simple doorway. The grander ones (for example no.
2 and no. 3) have an entrance vestibule with columns leading into
a grander interior hall, divided by columns into three bays, and
finally into a large niche which held the statue of the deceased.

Tomb no. 2 is the tomb of Ameni, whose biography and principal
exploits are inscribed on the entrance lintels; he took part in several
expeditions to the South with the King or Crown Prince; he
provided the temples with three thousand bulls with their cows;
when the Nile had an exceptionally favourable flood, he never
made it a pretext of increasing the taxes; all in all, he was an
excellent administrator.

The interior hall has been praised as achieving, both in architecture and decoration, the highest level of Egyptian art. The
decoration is in the form of wall-painting, much of it well preserved.
Very appealing are the scenes of the kitchen; pans repose on stoves,

the cook watches the pans, an assistant brings the meat. Very vivid are the scenes of war and strife. Wrestlers wrestle, boxers box, armies get under way, a fortress is attacked. What is remarkable about these scenes, by contrast to so much of what we shall see of Ancient Egypt, is the extraordinary freedom and naturalism of the scenes, reminiscent sometimes of the highest forms of the art of Greece. In more solemn mood we can admire, finally, near the terminal niche, scenes of pilgrimage to the two chief shrines of Osiris, a barge with the mummy of Ameni towed by two ships in full sail and a harem-boat towed by two ships with masts lowered.

It is thought that these tombs, or many of them, represent a dynasty of local potentates whose support was of importance to the Twelfth Dynasty Pharaohs. Tomb no. 3 is that of Khnemhotpe II, who is believed to be a nephew of Ameni. His tomb is less well preserved, but the record of his life survives and gives us once again the measure of his importance. While some of the interior architecture has disappeared, some of the painted decorations are remarkably preserved. Here again we see the daily life of Ancient Egypt, the carpenters, the weavers, the harvesters, the herdsmen and the fishermen; then the familiar hunting scenes and the voyage with the children and harem. But what is most remarkable in this tomb is the great tableau of the Asiatics, once thought to be Jacob and his family; a fascinating representation of the nomads of the desert as they presented themselves before the master four thousand years ago. The Pharaoh in question was apparently Sesostris II, builder of one of the pyramids in the Faiyum.

The difficulty in Ancient Egypt is always to avoid having too much of a good thing. Visitors with an appetite for more tombs might nevertheless be encouraged to visit no. 15, the tomb of Baket, and no. 17, the tomb of his son Kheti, monarch of the Antelope nome. In the wall paintings of these tombs we see, in addition to the familiar pictures, scenes of dancing and of desert hunts; birds and cattle; and in no. 15 an interesting social document, peasants forcibly brought in to declare their wealth for taxation purposes while the amounts are noted down by scribes. Not uninteresting, for those who have time, is a glance at the latest tombs, 35 to 39, the construction of which was never finished.

The sugar-factories decreed by Mehemet Ali in the nineteenth century have taken their toll of ancient masonry and some of these sites have been reduced to little more than mounds of rubble with protruding foundations of columns or of walls. On the right bank, reached from the small town of Roda, is the site of Antinoe or

Antinoopolis, a city built in the second century AD on the site of a
more ancient city in honour of Antinous the favourite of the Roman
Emperor Hadrian. A few miles to the south the amateur of Early
Christian relics may find near the village of El-Deir a small
subterranean Coptic church claiming an original foundation as
far back as the Empress Helena, mother of Constantine.

Malawi, the next considerable town, has preserved a certain
character and boasts a small museum filled somewhat haphazardly
with relics of local interest, largely supplied from the ancient
Hermopoulis. This site, reached from the left bank of the river,
was sacred to the god Thoth, two large statues of whom still stand
at the entrance, while ruins of his temple can be made out further
on. Another excursion can be made to Tonnal-el-Gebel, where can
be seen the enormous and extraordinary necropolis of the animals
sacred to Thoth, notably the monkey and the ibis. One of the
god's high-priests Petosiris, of about 300 BC and thus of the
Ptolemaic period, is commemorated in an impressive tomb preceded
by a long paved approach and decorated with elaborate reliefs, in
style partly Egyptian and partly Greek, in which the familiar scenes
of Egyptian life are varied by baboons, snakes, sacred bulls, hippopotami and crocodiles.

Another curious excursion, on the East bank, is to the Coptic
village of Deir-el-Barsha, with rock tombs including that of Dhuthotep of the period of the Twelfth Dynasty; it contains a remarkable
relief illustrating the transportation, on a sledge and without the
help of wheels, of a colossal statue some 21 feet in height.

Our next stop is Amarna. The city lay on the right or east side
of the Nile and formed a fairly narrow strip stretching from
north to south for a number of miles. Three main north-south
streets divided it, together with a number of streets intersecting at
right angles. The main features, inevitably, were the palaces and
the temples. The site is now reduced to the state of so many Egyptian
sites, heaps of rubble and rubbish with occasional protruding
remains. The determined visitor can nevertheless form for himself
a conception of what Amarna once was. The main palace lay south
of the modern village of El Tell and faced the Nile. The great
temple lay at right angles to it extending east and west. A smaller
temple lay to the south of it, behind the palace. A smaller palace,
again facing the Nile, lay some two miles to the north. Grand
mansions, factories, workshops, workmen's cottages filled the
enormous area. This was bounded, in a sort of semicircle fencing
it off from the desert, by the remarkable steles, a sequence of stone

pillars each about twelve feet high and inscribed with the royal instructions regarding the city limits. The two most remarkable finds in the city were the artists' houses and the Amarna tablets. Notable among the first was the house of the sculptor Thutmose, which contained the celebrated painted limestone bust of Akhenaten's Queen Nefertiti now in the Berlin museum. The Amarna tablets, now divided between Berlin, the British Museum and Cairo, provided an astonishing insight into the international relations of Egypt at this time; from them we have been able to read the views and ambitions of the Kings of Babylonia and Assyria and the reports of vassal princes from Syria, Tyre, Byblos and Jerusalem. But we must get back to the site.

The greatest survivals at the site, as so often in Egypt, are once more the tombs outside the city, of which there are two principal groups, the Northern and the Southern. Rock-tombs of the type which we have already seen so often, the Amarna tombs, are a considerable climb and, thanks to the damage they have suffered both in ancient and in modern times they are only of moderate interest. The dominating motifs are the sun-disc of Aten with his rays protruding downwards and the King and Queen themselves. Not the least interesting of the tombs are those which, on account of the fate which overtook the city on the Pharaoh's death, have been left incomplete. A full description (there are about twenty-five tombs in all) would be unbearably tedious, but it is worth making two points about their decoration as a whole. For here is a complete change from the usual visions of Ancient Egypt. No longer do the harvesters, shepherds, fishermen, workmen predominate; in the Amarna tombs, irrespective of the owners, what predominates is the Pharaoh, his Court and the particular religion which was the foundation of the whole enterprise. But what is also different is the style. Here the formality and rigidity of Ancient Egypt is suddenly relaxed; figures move and faces smile; the king and queen sit down to dinner while servitors prepare the food and drink and an orchestra regales them with music. Alas, that we cannot see within the mind of this lost world; the mystery becomes still greater when we look at the extraordinary sculptured features of the king found at Karnak and now in the Luxor Museum. At Amarna itself his face cannot be seen; all portraits of himself and his queen have been erased by the irate priests of Amun who after his death once more took over.

Fifty miles upstream from Amarna is Assiout, the largest modern town of Upper Egypt. We approach it through the lock of the Assiout dam, one of the earlier British projects for the regeneration of agricultural Egypt. Built in the years 1898-1902, it provides the starting point for the Ibrahimiya Canal which irrigates the provinces of Assoiut, Minya and Beni Suef. The town itself is by no means unattractive and forms a picturesque feature in the view from the surrounding heights. This may be sampled by those energetic enough to visit its Rock-Tombs. These appear to be of local princes flourishing during the Twelfth Dynasty and are of surprising extent; one of them, known as the Soldiers' Tomb, has become famous from its representation of rows of warriors armed with spears and large shields on the south wall of its pillared hall. The extraordinary mixture that is Egypt could hardly be better illustrated than here; a little further on is a Christian rock-chapel with Greek and Coptic inscriptions while extending out into the plain is an impressive Arab cemetery with literally hundreds of domed tombs.

The Nile valley south of Assiout continues to be littered with sites and relics of all ages of Egyptian history. Aboutig, a modern market town, has opposite it the village Tosa with an ancient necropolis. Sidfa, further on, is remarkable for its curious pigeon-houses in every shape and style of architecture. Tahta is opposite the heights which were haunted by a famous serpent, a worker of miracles, whose fame is said to be still extant among the modern inhabitants. Sohag is the base for the excursion to two very ancient Coptic establishments, the White Convent and the Red Convent. These are thought to have been built in the fourth or fifth century AD and thus take us back to the very earliest time of Christianity. It is easy, as one looks at the White Convent, to see what has happened to some of the buildings of Ancient Egypt; in the White Convent columns and pillars have been appropriated with little regard to suitability or size while some of the blocks of stone still carry their Ancient Egyptian hieroglyphics. More care was taken in the smaller Red Convent, with its matching capitals and columns. The White Convent houses a motley collection of inhabitants, men, women and children; it once housed also a large collection of Coptic manuscripts now dispersed to Western museums. The church, now crowned with a dome of later date, is interesting for its curious construction and a few surviving paintings, above all for its atmosphere of antique mystery.

South of Sohag we pass further ancient sites: Panopolis, now replaced by the modern Akhmim, remarkable in later ages for its reputation for loose morals and centre of much religious disputation and persecution; Ptolemais, now replaced by the modern El-Manchah, founded as its name implies by Ptolemy I and once one of the largest cities of Upper Egypt; Thinis, near Girga, thought to have been the capital of the First and Second Dynasties and not far from it a large brick mastaba thought to have been the tomb of King Zoser of the Third Dynasty. Girga itself, until displaced by Assiout, was once an important provincial capital. Ten miles south of Girga is Balliana, the base for the excursion to Abydos.

For the true Egyptologist there is no more interesting site than Abydos for it takes us to the very roots of Egyptian history. This starts inevitably with Osiris, the benevolent King-God of Ancient Egypt. By his enemies Osiris, as we have related, was not only slain but also cut into pieces which were distributed round the country; his head arrived at Abydos and here was solemnly buried. Abydos thus became the most sacred place in Egypt, a fact which was recognised as early as the First Dynasty, when King Zer chose it for his own tomb. Throughout the Old Kingdom a tremendous cult persisted; and if one could not actually be buried at Abydos, it was essential for one's prospects in the after-life that one should have some link. If one could not be buried there, one's body could be taken on a visit; if this was not possible, one could erect a stele; while easier still became the custom of depositing by way of personal memorial a votive cup, thousands of which accumulated over the centuries in this necropolis.

Osiris had of course his temple, built and rebuilt by successive Dynasties through the ages. The Pharaohs themselves ceased after a time to be buried here and the city went through many vicissitudes. A great new period of glory came with the Middle Kingdom; Senruset III, who built the pyramid at Dashur, had his first tomb here and great additions were made to the temple. But it was with the New Kingdom that the city reached its apogee. Rameses I, Seti I and Rameses II all contributed to do honour to Osiris and his sanctuary — a fact more remarkable when we think of the extent to which Thebes and Karnak had become by then the political and religious centres.

Fascinating though all this ancient pedantry may be for the Egyptologist, for the ordinary visitor the attraction of Abydos is of a very different kind. For the early relics have vanished, as so often, into mounds and rubbish heaps and there is a point beyond which the imagination can no more be taxed. But Abydos provides a sight for the eyes, the still surviving temples which the Pharaohs of the New Kingdom erected. Here for the first time on our Nile journey we can see in recognisable forms some of the tremendous structures erected in honour of the religion of Ancient Egypt.

The first is the temple of Seti I. The temples of Ancient Egypt vary greatly in plan but it is possible to list the main features which were basic to the idea. The entrance building is the Pylon, consisting of two great towers and a great gateway between them. This leads to a forecourt which is surrounded by a colonnade and which is therefore sometimes called the Peristyle Court. This in turn is followed by a second court with a central nave and side aisles filled with columns, which is called the Hypostyle Court. Finally the Sanctuary, with one or more shrines, usually flanked by rooms or chambers devoted to storage and the accessories of worship and ritual. These four parts are normally on a straight axis.

In the temple of Seti both the Pylon and the Peristyle Court are almost completely ruined and the entrance is thus straight into the Hypostyle Court. This is the first example of these constructions which make such an impression on the Egyptian traveller. One stands in a forest of gigantic stone columns, with clustered papyrus-bud capitals; too crowded, one might think in the space available and curiously ill-adapted for anything in the nature of congregational worship. Seti's temple has the peculiarity of a double Hypostyle Court. We enter a first Court with a double range of columns running transversely. Then through a wall with seven openings we reach the second Court, this time with a triple row of columns again running transversely. The first two rows have the papyrus-bud capitals; the third row has cylindrical columns with plain tops and stands at a higher level so as to give easy access to the Sanctuary.

Before entering the Sanctuary it is worth looking at some of the decorations in the two Halls. Though the temple was founded by Seti, it was completed by his son Rameses II and we are conscious of being in the presence of two contrasting styles of art. Rudiments of decoration survive in the ruins of the Peristyle Court; here we see Rameses II portrayed in various religious functions, as well as an enormous inscription recording his completion of the monument. There is more of Rameses II in the first part of the Hypostyle Court; Thoth and Horus pour holy liquid over the Pharaoh; the Pharaoh is conducted to the temple by gods with wolf head and falcon's head. Rameses hands an offering to Osiris and his companions Isis and Horus.

The sad thing about these reliefs is, not to put too fine a point on it, that they are mediocre. The greatest proportion of the art of Ancient Egypt which has survived is of the age of Rameses and most of it is of this quality. The contrast can be seen when we enter the second part of the Hypostyle Court and find ourselves in the presence of the art of Seti. Here the reliefs, though not of outstanding interest, are of outstanding quality; note, in particular, the admirable reliefs of the scenes on the north-west wall, where the Pharaoh himself is evidently portrayed from life and with the greatest skill.

From the Hypostyle Court we enter through seven entrances the Sanctuary with seven shrines. This in itself is peculiar, Egyptian temples in general being consecrated to one rather than several deities. Here Amun has occupied the centre, having usurped the place of Osiris who with other gods occupies five other shrines; while Seti himself has the easternmost shrine. The temple has a final peculiarity in that it turns at right angles into an easterly projection, consisting of a slaughter yard and a number of rooms. The most interesting of these is the Gallery of the Kings, so called from its famous list of Kings which enabled historians to deduce the succession of the Pharaohs from Menes down to Seti. It is noticeable that both Akhenaton and Queen Hatshepsut are omitted from the list.

What could have caused the temple-builders to make the right-angled turn at the Sanctuary could have been the Cenotaph now immediately behind the temple. Generally known as the Osireion, this structure appears in fact to be the Cenotaph of Seti himself. A long passage decorated with texts leads to an Anteroom and a Second Chamber; thence at right angles to a large Transverse Chamber beyond which is the principal Hall. This is a pillared hall in three aisles surrounded by a narrow passage from the outer side of which open a number of small chambers. The passage surrounds a kind of artificial island protected by a trench, in the middle of which are two cavities, one of them destined perhaps for Seti's tomb. The reliefs of Seti on the roof should not be missed.

The other monument of Abydos is the temple of Rameses II himself. The plan is the usual Egyptian one and the decorations, which are well preserved, are superior to most of those of Rameses. Sadly, the temple is badly ruined; nevertheless one can see in the Peristyle Court curious processions; a gazelle and a bull; soldiers responding to the call of the trumpet; prisoners of various nations and colours; a whole ceremony of sacrifice. On the outside walls

are spirited reliefs of the wars of Rameses with the Hittites. Like
Seti's temple, this temple had its Hypostyle Court, divided once
again into two parts.

About fifty miles upstream from Abydos is Dendera, the next
great monument of Ancient Egypt; on the way one passes the
strangely named Egplum, where with aid from Soviet Russia a
great complex is being developed for manufacturing aluminium.

Dendera was sacred to Hathor, a difficult goddess for she is
represented in many forms though usually at Dendera with woman's
head and cow's ears. She had a particular link with Horus, the
god whom we shall meet at Edfu.

The interest of Dendera is, first, that its temple is one of the
best preserved in Egypt and secondly that it is of very late date.
Nothing in Egyptian history is more extraordinary than the way
in which the Greek and Roman conquerors blandly accepted the
theocracy of Ancient Egypt with all its complications and adopted
it as their own. Sometimes efforts were made to identify with their
own gods; but principally the policy seems to have been to ally
with the gods of Egypt, the later rulers doing obeisance to them,
while they on the other hand contributed to flatter and exalt the
new rulers.

But Dendera, though its temple is, comparatively, of modern
date, is not a modern site. It is in fact one of the most ancient of
religious centres. But the oldest surviving structure, the so called
Birth-House (or Mammisi) of Nectanebo, is only of the Thirtieth
Dynasty, shortly antedating the Ptolemies. A second Birth-House,
of Roman times, lies near it and between them a remarkable Coptic
church thought to date from the fifth century AD. The other relics
at Dendera—the great temple apart—are a temple of Isis and a
sacred lake.

The great temple was building from the second century BC to
the second century AD. We enter through a great, but damaged,
gateway inscribed with the names of three Roman Emperors,
Domitian, Nerva and Trajan. Passing on the right the Birth-Houses
and the Coptic church, we reach the great courtyard and then the
façade of the Hypostyle Hall. Six huge Hathor-headed columns
confront us surmounted by a richly carved entablature and a great
cornice. Inside the Hall is a forest of similar columns, while the
walls are decorated with reliefs of the Roman age. The King or
Pharaoh or Emperor who is the central figure of these scenes is
discreetly anonymous; in them he goes through all the peripatetics
of the religion of Egypt and participates in ceremonies with many

of the ancient gods. The ceiling of the Hall is not without interest; a kind of panorama of astronomy covers it, with the signs of the zodiac, the winds, the months, the hours and of course the gods elaborately displayed.

In a civilisation whose art is remarkable for its unchanging styles, there are two features at Dendera that are worth noticing. First, the capitals of the great columns. These unusually are in two parts; the face of Hathor gazes out in four directions; above her head is a kind of square box with elegant reliefs. Secondly, the arrangement of the decoration on the temple walls. Here we are conscious of a decorative plan and symmetry which in most Egyptian decoration is strikingly absent; the interiors of the walls of the long sides of the halls are decorated with sunk reliefs, but the end walls have raised reliefs in four tiers of square panels which, being in scale with the height of the building, are both refined and effective. One gets the impression that after centuries of haphazard effort the interior decorator had at length arrived.

From the Hypostyle Hall we continue into a second and smaller Hypostyle Hall, flanked on each side by three service rooms and adorned with more reliefs in honour of the anonymous Pharaoh. Next comes the First Vestibule, which was used apparently for sacrifices, and then the Second Vestibule which enclosed the most sacred part of the temple, the Sanctuary. On the right of the Second Vestibule is the so-called Silver Room which leads to an open Court, used apparently for a special annual celebration of the birth of the god Horus, a celebration curiously reminiscent of the Christian Christmas. In the Sanctuary we see the Pharaoh burning incense before the two gods Hathor and Horus. Around it are eleven rooms or chambers, the central chamber immediately behind the Sanctuary being especially sacred to Hathor.

In both the Sanctuary and the Second Hypostyle Hall there is a continuation of the style of decoration on which we have already remarked. Unfortunately the darkness is such that one wonders if anyone can ever have derived much pleasure from it. What can be discerned in the Second Hypostyle Hall is a stranger type of capital; elongated downwards with floral reliefs the capitals make almost half the height of the columns.

The tour of the temple is completed by visits to the vaults and the roofs. There are twelve crypts and they have reliefs dating from the Eleventh Ptolemy by whom the present temple is thought to have been founded. Very grand reliefs also decorate the staircase by which one ascends to the roof. The theme is ingenious; the whole procession, standard bearers, hierophants, priests, king, move majestically upwards, accompanying the tourist on his ascent. The view is worth the climb.

On the outside of the temple the reliefs have historical interest. The south wall portrays not only the famous Cleopatra but also her son by Julius Caesar, Caesarion.

South of Dendera were other cities, Koptos and Ombos, now but heaps of ruins. We brace outselves for greater things as the Nile ship approaches Luxor.

9   LUXOR, KARNAK AND THEBES

Luxor is an important landmark for the traveller to Upper Egypt for although we have passed a number of towns, some much larger than Luxor, Luxor is the first which is in any way adapted for the reception and residence of the Western traveller. The enormous temples of Luxor and Karnak have always made it an obvious target for the sightseer and in the nineteenth century era when it became fashionable for the rich to escape the northern winter, the place was selected as an obvious winter resort. A number of hotels were accordingly built culminating in the ambitious Winter Palace.

It should not be thought that Luxor is like Monte Carlo. It has indeed the advantage of being very much warmer and for those who enjoy sight-seeing there is much more to see. But although hotels have been built for the Westerner, the town remains totally un-Westernised. It still pursues the Arab way of life, with Arab voices, Arab noises and sometimes Arab dirt, and the only agreeable walk is along the Nile boulevard. It is also not a large town; when one goes shopping there is nothing comparable with the great souks of Damascus or Aleppo, nothing comparable with the great bazaar of Cairo; trading is done in little unpretentious shops and not on the basis of fixed prices but of skilled bargaining. Apart from the great sightseeing excursions there is little to do except ride round the town in a horse-carriage or take a trip in a sailing-boat on the Nile.

The modern town is on the east or right bank. Here also are the great temples of Luxor and Karnak, situated some two miles apart. On the other bank of the Nile is a wide strip of cultivation and beyond it where the cultivation ends is the famous City of the Dead. The modern town occupies only a fraction of the area of the ancient city on the East bank, let alone the City of the Dead. No one knows why or how the place acquired the Greek name of Thebes. Originally a small provincial capital, it began to rise to importance in the time of the Middle Kingdom and its local god Amun began to be known. After the disastrous epoch of the Hyskos it apparently became the base for the reconquest or re-uniting of the whole country and it displaced or rivalled Memphis as the Egyptian capital. Its greatest period was under the New Kingdom when successive Pharaohs contributed to the enormous buildings which survive today. With the growth of the buildings grew the power of the priests; Amun became the greatest deity of Egypt; and eventually the priests were able to rule the kings. The result was a decadence continuing through the centuries; disaster struck at the time of the Persian invasion when the city was sacked. A partial recovery followed but the inhabitants had a death wish; successive revolts were organised under the Ptolemies and the Romans, repressions followed and by the Christian era the city life had virtually finished. Strabo, who visited it about 20 BC, found only scattered villages on the ancient site.

It is not easy at a distance of thousands of years to understand why and how the great capital of Egypt under the New Kingdom acquired or required two gigantic temples of the size of Luxor and Karnak. Rome has its four large Christian basilicas, London has its Westminster Abbey and St Paul's Cathedral, Constantinople its Santa Sofia and its Suleimaniye mosque. Causes that we cannot now identify must have had the same effect in ancient Thebes. Karnak was the first to be begun, by the first Pharaohs of the Eighteenth Dynasty. Most of the Pharaohs from Ahmose I onwards contributed a share, and a major contribution was made by Amenophis III. This was the Pharaoh who, simultaneously and for very political reasons, embarked on the great project of Luxor. Possibly he viewed Karnak as a state temple and Luxor as his personal temple. But we are only speculating.

Founded by Amenophis III, the temple of Luxor dates from an earlier epoch than Abydos or Dendera. Like many other buildings of Ancient Egypt, the temple had a practical purpose, to consolidate the claim of the Pharaoh to the throne of Egypt, a measure made necessary by the fact that, though the son of a Pharaoh, Amenophis was on his mother's side very far from royal. The method adopted was to substitute for his human ancestry a religious or divine ancestry from the god who had now become supreme in Egypt, Amun-Re. To this theory the great temple and its elaborate reliefs are accordingly dedicated. It was his son Akhenaten, whom we have encountered at Amarna, who reacted against the whole cult of Amun-Re. At Luxor he built a new shrine within the temple to his own god Aten and did his best to expunge the earlier cult. His successors reverted to the older faith and Luxor entered a further period of glory.

The temple of Amenophis had the familiar sequence; great pylon, forecourt, hypostyle hall, first vestibule, second vestibule, sanctuary. A modern entrance has been made into the western side of the forecourt, which ranks among the finest productions of Egyptian architecture. It is almost a square, surrounded on three sides by double rows of clustered papyrus-bud columns. The hypostyle hall beyond it is a rectangle with thirty-two columns arranged in four rows. Beyond this the temple has been altered since its original construction; the first vestibule was converted in early Christian times into a Christian church, while part of the sanctuary had previously been converted into a chapel by Alexander the Great. The reliefs here are of Alexander's period but in the so-called Birth Room beyond the first vestibule we revert to Amenophis and to the temple's original *raison d'être*, the walls being copiously adorned with reliefs illustrating the Pharaoh's divine ancestry, a theme which is continued in the chambers which form the temple's southern end.

The temple has at its northern end a prelude almost as remarkable as the temple itself. North of the great pylon which formed the original entrance there has been projected, possibly by Amenophis, possibly by his successors, a great colonnaded hall elaborately adorned with representations of the great religious festivals in honour of Amun-Re. And beyond this hall we find yet another addition, a great forecourt built a century later by Rameses II and now partly appropriated by a Moslem mosque.

Not the least remarkable feature of Luxor is the great Pylon which precedes this last forecourt. Two obelisks, some seventy feet high, stood in front of it. In the year 1831 they were presented by Mehemet Ali in a fit of generosity to the French nation which with singular moderation accepted only one of the pair, transporting it in 1833 to the Place de la Concorde. The survivor remains and is a considerable work of art, being adorned with pictures of Rameses II and Amun-Re, with finely incised inscriptions. The Pylon was further remarkable for the six colossal statues which fronted it; two seated statues of the Pharaoh survive to right and left, while one of the other four remains to show the Pharaoh in the full splendour of a standing position. On the Pylon itself are engraved the scenes, which become so familiar in Ancient Egypt, of the campaigns and battles of Rameses II with the Hittites of Asia Minor.

The alterations of later ages have obliterated the original plan of Amenophis the essence of which was the uniting of the temple of Luxor with the much larger temple of Karnak in a single monumental layout. Situated nearly two miles apart, the two tei..iples were joined originally by a triumphal way lined with monumental sphinxes and following roughly the course of the modern road up to the pylon entrance of Amenophis. Vestiges still survive and can be identified, but the main effect of the monumental scheme has been obliterated by the centuries.

To get to Karnak from Luxor we must take a commonplace modern street.

Karnak consists now of a number of smallish temples disposed around its greatest and most famous structure, the great temple of Amun. A small part survives of the triumphal approach of Amenophis and we may walk between lines of sphinxes—the so-called Western Avenue—to the temple of Khons. The temple is preceded by a handsome portal erected in the third century BC by Euergetes, one of the Ptolemies, and forming the south-west entrance to the precinct of Karnak.

Khons was the moon-god of Egypt and was the son of Amun and Mut. His temple is due to the Twentieth Dynasty, having being founded about 1180 BC by Rameses III and terminated some hundred years later. An impressive pylon survives and beyond it the habitual Court, Hypostyle Hall and Sanctuary. Reliefs and painting also survive from many centuries including even the Roman; most significant perhaps are those of Herihor, the priest king who followed the Rameses and founded the Twenty-First Dynasty. At right angles to this temple is the smaller temple of Epet.

The great temple of Amun is built at right angles to the Nile and so lies roughly east and west. A large addition to it projects southwards. Rude things have been said about it but no one has ever managed to talk down its size and scale. It is in fact, even in its present partly ruined state, the world's largest religious building and it has been estimated that within its area it could without difficulty accommodate St Paul's in London, Notre Dame de Paris and St Peter's in Rome. Only once, we are asked to believe, was there ever a building which was even greater, the now vanished Labyrinth whose site we have noted in the Faiyum.

The building of the temple was spread over a thousand years but in the main the credit is due to the Pharaohs of the New Kingdom (Eighteenth and Nineteenth Dynasties) starting with Ahmose I about the year 1580 BC. So large is the structure that it is divided into nine or ten separate portions each provided with its individual pylon. Starting from the temple of Khons we reach the western end of the temple at Pylon No. 1.

Pylon No. 1 is thought to be the creation of Sheshonk, a Pharaoh of the Twenty-Second Dynasty, or of Tahaska of the Twenty-Fifth. Its size and scale set the tone for the scenes to come: 370 feet wide, 50 feet thick and 142 feet high, it easily dwarfs such structures as the West front of St Paul's cathedral. From its summit is a notable view, a forest of halls and pillars extending eastwards along the route we are about to take.

Next comes the great Forecourt, a creation again of the Twenty-Second Dynasty embracing as mere details two structures which in any other setting would be important monuments in their own right; on the left, the Temple of Seti and on the right the Temple of Rameses III. The siting of the latter, breaking as it does through the Forecourt wall, gives a clue to the architectural history by showing that the great temple was intended originally to terminate east of the Forecourt and that its further extension necessitated the incorporation of the Rameses temple into the final scheme. Across the Forecourt we approach what was thus the original entrance to the great temple, now the Second Pylon of Rameses I. Much ruined though this Pylon is, we can still admire the gigantic portal and to the right of it, in the so-called Portico of the Bubastides, the famous relief of Sheshonk triumphing over Judah and Israel.

Admiration becomes stupefaction as we pass through the portal and enter the Hypostyle Hall. 136 gigantic columns carry a sandstone roof which in the centre aisle is 79 feet above the floor. Many obvious criticisms have been made of the general effect; but it has also had remarkable praise. 'The Pyramids', says one authority, 'are more stupendous. The Colosseum covers more ground. The Parthenon is more beautiful. Yet in nobility of conception, in vastness of detail, in majesty of the highest order, the Hall of Pillars exceeds them every one.' Another authority by contrast says: 'The only special feature of this hall is its great defect—that the columns are far too numerous.... The size which strikes us is not the grandeur of strength but the bulkiness of disease.' It is necessary before making comparisons to remind ourselves of the purpose of the building. Egyptian temples were not built for congregational worship; the need for open interior space and unhindered visibility which dominates the design of Christian cathedrals was wholly lacking. There was thus no practical objection to the close spacing of the columns. Was the temple hall designed as a thing of beauty? If so, it is to our eyes a failure. Perhaps it was built only to the glory and majesty of the god and if so it becomes intelligible. Alternatively, the architects may have decided on purely structural grounds that the only safe way of supporting the enormous sandstone roof was by close spacing of enormous columns. Some idea of their size can be visualised by the estimate that a hundred men could stand on the great capital which each column supports. The area covered — and this is only a small part of the whole temple — is about the same area as Canterbury Cathedral. Egypt has many wonders and perhaps once had many more; of those which survive this hall is the ultimate achievement in monumental building. It is perhaps preferable not to criticise or compare; better to align oneself with the poet who, contemplating another imaginary masterpiece of architecture, summarised his own thoughts: 'Look on my works, Ye Mighty, and despair.'

Seti I and Rameses II, both of the Nineteenth Dynasty, are thought to be the Pharaohs primarily responsible for this hall and much of their history is recorded in reliefs both in the interior and on the exterior walls, Seti on the north wall and Rameses on the south. We view again, inevitably, the war of Rameses II against the Hittites; more interesting, from its Biblical associations, is the triumphal inscription of Sheshonk at the western end of the south wall, commemorating once again his triumph over Judah and Israel.

The Hypostyle Hall ends with the Third Pylon built by Amenophis III and now much ruined. This gives into a Central Court which in effect divides the whole temple into two parts. A notable survival here is an obelisk of red Assuan granite, one of the lightest obelisks of the ancient world; it is attributed to Tuthmosis I, an early Pharaoh of the Eighteenth Dynasty.

The second half of the temple begins with the Fourth Pylon, also much ruined. Beyond this in what was originally a colonnade survives a much grander obelisk, also from Assuan and said to be the highest of all ancient obelisks with the exception of that at the Lateran; the attribution this time is to Queen Hatshepsut, a lady Pharaoh who will make several more appearances in our exploration of Thebes.

A Fifth Pylon and a Sixth Pylon lead through and into a more complicated part of the building, for we have here entered the area which had been first built in the Middle Kingdom and later adapted as a component element of the great temple. Beyond the Fifth Pylon on the left is a colossal statue of Amenophis II. Beyond the Sixth Pylon is the so-called Hall of Records to which a number of Pharaohs apparently contributed, including the well known name of Tutankhamen; it was he apparently who symbolised the return of the ancient religion after the apostasy of Akhenaten by installing the colossal statue of Amun. A granite chapel which adjoins was an intrusion of Ptolemaic times.

Queen Hatshepsut makes herself evident again in the section which follows, and here we see the first evidence of the long feud which apparently divided her from her successors Tuthmosis II and Tuthmosis III. The method adopted was to delete her portraits from all the reliefs and paintings of her reign, sometimes substituting for them portraits of her successors. Reliefs in this condition can be seen in the chambers north and south of the Hall of Records, those in the north chamber being particularly fine.

We now emerge into an open courtyard, in which it is thought the main part of the Middle Kingdom temple stood, and beyond it into the great festal temple of Tuthmosis III. Though not comparable in size with the great Hypostyle Hall, this may be regarded as the Second Wonder of Karnak consisting as it does of a great roofed rectangular space with five aisles divided by square columns and pillars representing tent poles. The King himself stands guard outside the entrance and in a chapel within he is to be seen in a colossal group with the gods Amun and Mut. The Sanctuary, which was the culmination of this great building on its central axis, is entered from the east side of Tuthmosis' Hall.

A great girdle wall built probably by Rameses II surrounds the eastern half of the great temple. Immediately against it at its eastern end and thus almost adjoining the Sanctuary is Tuthmosis' mortuary chapel in which, united in death as not in life, are to be seen colossal seated figures of the Pharaoh and Queen Hatshepsut; while preceding it is a pillared hall containing colossal statues of the Pharaoh portrayed as the god Osiris.

Before completing the visit to the southward extension of the great temple with its remaining Pylons, an excursion may be made northwards from the Hypostyle Hall to the Temple of Ptah and the Temple of Mont. Of the temple of Mont, who was the local war-god of Thebes, very little remains, but the temple of Ptah is in tolerable preservation and records a remarkable variety of Pharaohs and periods. Amenemmes I of the Twelfth Dynasty is commemorated here; Tuthmosis III is much in evidence; some of the gateways are due to Shabako of the Twenty-Fifth Dynasty; and the Ptolemies have left their mark. Its most famous feature is the black granite statue of lion-headed goddess Sekhmet, once renowned on account of a supposed infinity of malevolent powers.

The sequence of pylons of the great temple continues southwards at right angles from the Central Court. Through an open court one comes to the Seventh Pylon, much ruined, and then to the Eighth Pylon, attributed respectively to Tuthmosis and Hatshepsut and remarkable for some colossal red granite statues of Pharaohs of the Middle and New Kingdoms. Pylon Eight is better preserved than Pylon Seven and is adorned with numerous reliefs from which as usual Hatshepsut's own portraits have been chiselled out. The Ninth and Tenth Pylons were built by Haremhab, last Pharaoh of the Eighteenth Dynasty. The Tenth Pylon served as the monumental entrance to the Southern extension of the great temple. It was approached by another avenue of sphinxes some of which survive; the avenue leads us to the well preserved and picturesque Temple of Mut.

The other temples which surrounded the great temple of Amun are mostly ruined or in poor condition. But it is perhaps worth giving a glance to the site of the Sacred Lake, the rectangular shape of which can still be made out on the south side of the second half of the great temple. It is also worth penetrating to the preserved East gate of the Girdle Wall some 500 yards from the First Pylon. Built by Nectanebis, a Pharaoh of the Thirtieth Dynasty about 370 BC, it marks the limit of the great Karnak complex and from it one can trace part of the bounding wall.

No records survive of the size of the priesthood and personnel needed to service this enormous religious centre. But records do survive which proclaim, accurately or not, their wealth and power. Amun is said at one moment to have possessed 5,164 divine statues, 81,322 slaves, vassals and servants, 421,262 head of cattle, 691,334 acres of land, 83 ships, 46 building yards and 65 cities and towns; in the temple were 5,164 divine images and a total of 86,486 statues. Some credence to these figures was provided by the discovery early in the present century, in what was apparently a store for unused objects near the Seventh Pylon, of over 700 stone statues, 7 sphinxes, 5 statues of sacred animals and over 17,000 bronzes. These statistics, uninteresting in themselves, give some idea of the scale and size of the priestly establishment which was challenged by Akhenaten when he removed his capital to Amarna and abandoned the cult of Amun as he thought forever.

Great as is the interest of the City of the Living at Thebes, a much greater challenge is presented by the City of the Dead. This is the huge area on the Left Bank of the Nile devoted to the tombs of the Pharaohs and their more important subjects and to their funeral temples. With the discovery in the year 1922 of the Tomb of Tutankhamen world fame was achieved for the Valley of the Kings. This, though in a sense the most important centre of interest, is really no more than a detail in the whole area which comprises, in addition to the Valley of the Kings, the Valley of the Queens, five separate areas of tombs of important citizens, four outstandingly important funeral temples (out of a number of others) and the famous Colossi of Memnon. It is thought that in ancient times the City of the Dead was also regularly inhabited by the living, including the priests, the administrators of the tombs, the workmen and often relatives of the deceased—somewhat on the model of the Tombs of the Caliphs and the Tombs of the Mamelukes in modern Cairo. The whole gigantic undertaking, like Luxor and Karnak themselves, was due to the Pharaohs of the New Kingdom from the Eighteenth to the Twenty-First Dynasties and though numerous other gods participated, it was primarily a glorification of the cult of Amun.

Hundreds of tombs have been discovered and more still will be discovered in years to come. So that to make a detailed inspection of this Dead City would be a labour of many days or weeks under the unvarying Egyptian sun. For the ordinary visitor a rigid selectivity must be the rule, but it is not so easy to prescribe a route or sequence in which the selected sites should be seen. One must resign oneself to chance or the dictates of the tourist agency, who must also organise the necessary automobiles, tractors, camels, horses, donkeys and soft drinks.

Nearest to the usual landing stage is the Funeral Temple of Seti I, the first of the great Pharaohs of the Nineteenth Dynasty, son of Rameses I and father of Rameses II. Seti's work we have already admired at Abydos and what remains of his work here deserves equal praise. Unfortunately much of his temple has perished and of what remains part is the less distinguished work of his son. The first two courts with their pylons have gone but the further core of the temple remains, together with a distinguished colonnade of papyrus columns which precedes the Hypostyle Hall. Compared with what we have seen at Karnak, this is a diminutive affair, but architecturally it is more distinguished; beyond it comes the Sanctuary and a third chamber and on each side a bewildering variety of partly ruined rooms and storehouses. Amun, obviously, figures largely in the decorations which are chiefly concerned with Seti and his son making offerings to a variety of gods.

North west of the Temple of Seti is the Necropolis called Drah

Abon el Neggah, partly in foothills and partly in plain. The most remarkable of these tombs is probably that of Amenmose, first prophet in the time of Rameses I and Seti I. The decorations, although essentially religious in character, portray a remarkable variety of scenes, the boat of Osiris, the palanquin of Amenophis I and the arrival of a funeral boat at Karnak with its great pylon and flags visible in the background.

The route continues to Deir-el-Bahari, with one of the most sensational monuments of the Dead City, the Temple of Hatshepsut.

We have already encountered Hatshepsut, but her story, so far as it can be reconstructed, is worth telling in more detail. Daughter of the Eighteenth Dynasty Pharaoh Tuthmosis I, she found herself married to one of her father's bastards Tuthmosis II, but revenged herself by producing only daughters. The solution once again was to marry one of the daughters to a bastard of the father, the young Tuthmosis III. The arrangement did not commend itself to Hatshepsut, who on her husband's death seized supreme power and maintained herself for twenty-two years against the pretensions of her son-in-law. The latter revenged himself on her death by dating his reign from his father's death and by obliterating wherever possible the portraits and memorials of his predecessor. Her mortuary temple, however he could not destroy.

Hatshepsut was not the first builder on this remarkable site. Mentuhotep II and III of the Eleventh Dynasty had a temple here and vestiges of it survive. But the scene is dominated by the successive colonnades which were the creation of Senmut, the architect of the Queen. Senmut conceived the temple on three levels with two great courtyards, connected with each other and with the temple proper by imposing ramps; and though much is destroyed the two great colonnades in the main survive. The left-hand portion of the second colonnade is famous for its representations of the Land of Punt. This is thought to be Somaliland and the pictures, though sadly deteriorated, provide an interesting record of a peaceful mission to that country during the Queen's reign. To the left of the Punt Colonnade is another colonnade leading to the Shrine of the goddess Hathor where Hatshepsut (usually defaced) appears in a number of strange ceremonies with the Hathor cow. In the corresponding chapel of Anubis on the other side some good colouring has survived particularly in the ceiling decoration. The Upper Court, which is the concluding stage of the temple, is largely ruined though some of its lateral rooms may be seen; the temple terminates in a long narrow sanctuary which appears to have been added to in Ptolemaic times. Scenically this temple is the finest thing in the City of the Dead.

It was in a cachette not far from this temple that Maspero made in 1881 one of the most astonishing discoveries in the history of Egyptology. Here, piled one on top of the other in the utmost confusion, were mummies of the Pharaohs from the Seventeenth to the Twenty-First Dynasties, together with numerous queens and princesses—vivid evidence of the difficulty found, even in ancient times, of preventing tomb robberies and of the desperate measures thought necessary to give the royal personages their chance of civilised living in the world of the dead.

The famous Valley of the Kings, which lies to the north west of the Temple of Hatshepshut, appears to have been originally selected as the royal resting place by Tuthmosis I of the Eighteenth Dynasty. By 1976 sixty-two tombs had been found, four of which are in the so-called Western Valley. The theme of the decorations, which vary greatly in elaboration though little in style, is always the same—the welfare of the Deceased in the World to Come. The sacred place in every case is the terminal chapel and this will be preceded by a greater or lesser underground chamber, connected sometimes by corridors of considerable length.

The approach to the Valley is not the least impressive part. The new tarmac road winds behind a mound of rubbish into what seems like a lost world. Golden-brown slopes and cliffs block or frame the view on every side as the road, twisting, climbing and turning, penetrates steadily into an increasingly complicated mountain complex. Finally we arrive at a small opening where a Tourist Rest House provides a welcome local landscape.

The tombs are situated in all directions around this feature. Long since despoiled by tomb robbers, they remained neglected and forgotten until in the early nineteenth century curiosity and cupidity once more took over. The early outrages of the new tomb-robbers are now forgiven and forgotten; discipline and dignity have taken their place; and this astonishingly difficult sight-seeing area is presented for the tourist in a manner which combines restraint with intelligence and good taste.

Tuthmosis' own tomb, though his sarcophagus still survives, is too ruinous to permit a visit. His grandson Tuthmosis III is grandly commemorated in a tomb culminating in a large hall with curved corners; his sarcophagus remains, the lid beside it broken in pieces, his mummy among those discovered by Maspero. Even grander is the tomb of his son Amenophis II. Here, after a long descent of ramps and more than ninety steps through a long series of ante-chambers we penetrate to an immense hall, now set out for the visitor in a way which makes it one of the most distinguished of all the tombs of Egypt. Glass panels and skilfully concealed lighting show off to excellent advantage one of the best designed decorative schemes of the New Kingdom. The hall is upheld by four square free-standing pillars supporting a roof some fifteen or twenty feet high. Their four faces are decorated with life-size scenes of gods and Pharaohs, all on religious themes and proportioned to the height of the hall. The walls by contrast are divided horizontally into a scheme of three panels running right round the hall and decorated as it were as an immense unrolled papyrus with text and illustrations of the Book of the Next World. A ceiling of blue and gold completes the scheme, which terminates at a lower level in the tomb chamber proper. Here one may gaze down upon the granite sarcophagus incised with black and gold which, until its removal to the Cairo museum in 1934, still held the body of the Pharaoh.

At the end of the Eighteenth Dynasty and after the interlude of Akhenaten we come to Tutankhamen.

The fame of Tutankhamen derives from the fact that in all the history of Egyptology his is the only royal tomb which has been discovered virtually undisturbed and in its original state. The tomb thus owed its fame to its contents rather than its structure and since the contents have been removed for safety to the Cairo Museum, the tomb is not comparatively speaking of major interest. A visit to it is nevertheless a must.

The tomb is small and what is difficult to imagine after seeing the immense display in the Cairo Museum is how this vast collection was ever packed into so confined a space. What has been left in place is the sarcophagus itself containing the King's mummy in the largest of its magnificent gold coffins. What is also satisfying is the decor of life-size figures of the Pharaohs and the gods which lines the walls.

With the Nineteenth Dynasty we come to the tomb of Seti I, the most remarkable in the Valley of the Kings. More than a hundred steps and no less than seven corridors and antechambers precede the main hall where stood the great sarcophagus found empty by Belzoni in 1815 and transported strangely to England to form part of the Soane collection in Lincoln's Inn Fields; the royal mummy was another of those discovered by Maspero in the cachette near Deir el Bahari: while other trophies from the tomb have found their way to Florence or to the Louvre. The tomb by no means finished at the main hall; two chambers lie beyond it and at many points the main corridor is flanked with lateral rooms. Considered as a whole, this enormous tomb nowhere achieves the dignity and unity of the main hall of the tomb of Amenophis II but in the complexity of its rooms and corridors the decorations achieve much greater variety and a serious study of them, even by the tourist, would be a matter of several hours. The walls generally speaking are paintings or raised reliefs, while the ceilings are painted on flat stone. There is evidence that even at its present size the scheme of the tomb was not complete and that further extensions were intended. The imagination boggles at the resources of human skill and labour required to produce what we see today.

The tomb of his great successor Rameses II is too dilapidated to be visible; but of the later Rameses, that of Rameses III is well preserved and even that of Rameses VI is worth a visit. A lengthy succession of rooms and corridors constitutes the tomb of Rameses III, some of them profusely and minutely inscribed with the sacred books of Egypt; the long sequence leads eventually to the burial chamber and the fate of the Egyptian royal tombs could not be more vividly illustrated; the mummy was one of those found by Maspero in the cachette near Deir-el-Bahari, the sarcophagus is in the Louvre while the lid resposes, inconsequently, in the Fitzwilliam Museum at Cambridge.

Rameses VI appears to have appropriated an earlier tomb and to have extended it to hold his own sarcophagus. A comparatively shallow affair, it provides an easy visit for the tiring tourist, descending through shallow levels to a sequence of rooms and corridors with decorations often sadly damaged. The tomb lid and broken parts of the sarcophagus survive in the terminal chamber, the striking feature of which is the ceiling brilliantly coloured and decorated in an artistic design of blue and gold.

South of Hatshepsut's Temple at Deir-el-Bahari are the three considerable tomb areas known as Assassif, Khoka and Cheik Abd el Gournah. These are the tombs of the officials, high and low, priests, dignitaries and grandees of the New Kingdom. Generally they do not vie in scale with the royal tombs and they were built with different objects. As between themselves they vary enormously in size, scale, shape, decoration and state of preservation. Though some of them have religious scenes, particularly connected with the funeral rites of the deceased, the principal interest of their decorations, as so often in Egyptian tombs, is in the picture they give of daily life in its infinitely varied aspects. In the area of Cheik Abd el Gournah the tomb of Nakht, an official and priest of Amun under the Eighteenth Dynasty, has well-preserved paintings showing all the stages of the Ancient Egyptian harvest, followed by scenes of the deceased and his wife seated at table and receiving sequences of gifts, while unobserved under their chair a cat is silently devouring a morsel of fish. The tomb of Menna in the same area is perhaps more typical of the tombs as a whole, space being given to domestic and agricultural scenes with some spirited sequences of hunting, fishing and shooting with bow and arrow, but a greater emphasis on funeral and religious ceremonies. An impressive tomb is that of Ramose, vizier of the Pharaoh Amenophis III; originally it contained a large hall with thirty-two reliefs, some of them possibly intruded in the Amarna period, with an impressive display of ladies' wigs.

Below these tomb areas is the famous Rameseum, the funeral temple of Rameses II. Already famous in ancient times when it was described by Diodorus under the name of Osimandias, the Rameseum has survived only moderately well the hazards of the centuries but is still a major sight-seeing object on the Theban tour. The original design was two great courtyards, each preceded by a Pylon and leading to a Hypostyle Hall, followed by smaller halls of the same type and the Sanctuary and flanked by a large assortment of ancillary chambers. Much of the first entrance Pylon survives and on the interior side we see those scenes with which we become so wearily familiar in many of the monuments of Rameses, the story of his wars with the Hittites and in particular the battle of Kadesh. Outside the second Pylon are the broken relics of one of Rameses' seated statues estimated in its original form to have been over fifty feet high and to have weighed more than a thousand tons. The principal remaining relics are the columns of the Hypostyle Hall of which twenty-nine are still erect.

After the Rameseum comes Deir-el-Medina, which includes another area of tombs, a Ptolemaic temple and the workmen's village. The temple, built by Ptolemy IV Philopator, is small but graceful; its principal interest is in the fact that it appears to be completely unaltered and in its original state. Hathor seems to be the presiding goddess and seven heads of her are to be seen over the doorway entrance to the central chapel; and some capitals with rich foliage carving provide a refreshing change from the generality of Egyptian capitals. The tombs are mostly in a poor state and for those with limited time can perhaps be omitted; the best is probably the tomb of Peshedu where some of the coloured decoration has been unusually well preserved. The workman's village, though of no architectural or artistic interest, is worth more than a passing glance. It is an area of walls, floors and foundations representing, incredibly, the houses lived in by the workmen who toiled at the construction of these tombs and temples so many centuries ago.

West of Deir-el-Medina is the Valley of the Queens, the name given to a tomb-area which, in addition to the wives of the Pharaohs, was apparently the burial-area of other members of the Pharaohs' families. We wind our way up into a valley with scenery comparable to, though less grand than, the Valley of the Kings; at a number of points one can look back and enjoy a splendid view of the cultivated area where once stood the left-bank city of Thebes with the Colossi of Memnon which we shall shortly visit. The tombs are not on the same scale as the tombs of the Pharaohs but some of them have well preserved their coloured decoration, notably the tomb of Prince Kha-em-weset, son of Rameses III. Queen Titi (it is not known whose wife she was) has a tolerably preserved tomb, though here the decorations have suffered; they are better preserved in the tomb of Khamonost, thought to be another son of Rameses III, and better still in the tomb of yet another son Amon-her-Khopechef. The show-piece of this tomb-area used to be the tomb of Queen Nefertari, wife of Rameses II; at the time of writing it is unfortunately closed due to the urgent need for remedial works to prevent it from collapse; the plan, we are told, is almost on the scale of a Pharaoh's tomb, consisting of a sequence of corridor and chambers excellently decorated with painted stucco reliefs.

Before returning to Luxor a very worthwhile diversion is to Medinet Habu. This is the name given to an area which appears to have been principally the creation of the Pharaoh Rameses III and to have comprised temples, palaces and a considerable village or town. What principally now survives is Rameses' great temple, but south of it are interesting relics of a number of other buildings, in particular the Royal Pavilion. This is a kind of triumphal entrance gate built apparently on a Syrian model and is thought to have been inspired by the fortresses encountered by the Pharaoh on his Asiatic campaigns. Like all the buildings of Rameses III it is a glorification of his military campaigns and the walls are profusely adorned with pictures of the Pharoah and tutelary gods and in particular the Asiatic prisoners brought back from the wars. Medinet Habu has, almost without exaggeration, acres of incised reliefs; when we come to the temple, it is worth looking for the relief of the bull hunt and the relief of the naval battle. Two courtyards of the temple survive in fairly good preservation; notice in the first courtyard the columns on one side with their 'umble' capitals and on the other side the square pillars faced with colossal statues. The second courtyard, with square pillars on its long sides and columns with bud capitals on its short sides, is very dignified; the hypostyle hall beyond is too ruined to be impressive. Remarkable all over this temple (and the decorations carry on outside as well as inside the walls) is the depth of the incised reliefs; the advantage of this technique was to make it more difficult for a jealous successor to excise them and substitute his own.

The return to Luxor can conveniently be made past the Colossi of Memnon.

> *I met a traveller from an antique land*
> *Who said: Two vast and trunkless legs of stone*
> *Stand in the desert. Near them, on the sand*
> *Half sunk, a shattered visage lies whose frown,*
> *And wrinkled lip, and sneer of cold command...*

So wrote the poet Shelley. These immensely impressive stone figures in fact stand not in the desert but in the cultivated land now covering the site of ancient Thebes. In Greek and Roman times they were apparently the sightseers' favourite target out of all the antiquities of Egypt and they are covered with an amazing number of graffiti dating from those times. Their name they owed to the Greeks; in historical fact they were twin statues of the Pharaoh Amenophis III erected in front of his mortuary temple which has now practically disappeared. The northern colossus became a particular tourist attraction in Roman times when, after being damaged by an earthquake, it began to emit a musical note at sunrise and it is recorded that the emperor Hadrian paid a special visit to hear it. A later emperor, Septimius Severus decided to repair the statue; the result was fatal; the statue never sang again.

Back in Luxor and before leaving it, one must repair one omission and visit the Museum. This is a small but beautifully laid-out collection in a building on the Nile-side and should most certainly be seen. Its principal interest for the specialist is the so-called Wall of the Tolatates, a collection of blocks of stone brought from a temple built by Akhenaten at Thebes with portraits of the Pharaoh, his queen and their special god, followed by an interesting series of scenes of many of the artifacts of Egypt. Upon the ordinary visitor some of the portrait busts will make a greater impression; Tuthmosis III is here, five foot high in basalt; in black granite is the portrait bust of Amenhotep, architect of Amenophis III; there is a marble sphinx four foot long. But the most enduring memory will surely be the two sandstone heads of the ever-mysterious Akhenaten himself; Shelley never saw them, but never has a sculptor better expressed 'the sneer of cold command.'

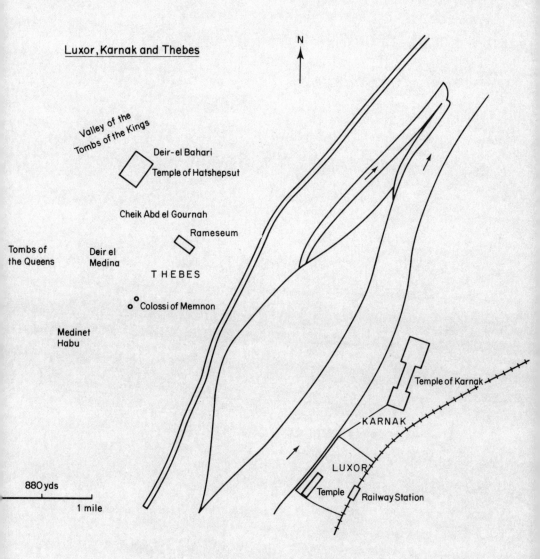

Luxor, Karnak and Thebes

N

Valley of the
Tombs of the Kings

Deir-el Bahari
Temple of Hatshepsut

Cheik Abd el Gournah

Rameseum

Tombs of   Deir el
the Queens   Medina

T H E B E S

Colossi of Memnon

Medinet
Habu

Temple of Karnak

KARNAK

LUXOR

Temple   Railway Station

880 yds

1 mile

10 FROM LUXOR TO ABU SIMBEL

A few miles south of Luxor is the small town of Esna, one of the more congenial of Upper Egypt. It is preceded by the Esna barrage built about the year 1906; an impressive piece of early twentieth-century engineering, it makes possible the irrigation of a large part of the province of Qena.

The town encloses a temple which in any other country would be called large but which by Egyptian standards is small and compact. It illustrates vividly two of the oddest aspects of Egyptology. What Ancient Egypt was, what happened to it and how it has been retrieved can be well understood by gazing down from street level into the large hole where the temple now stands. The inscriptions of Bonaparte's soldiers are on the roof, which is explained by the fact that during the centuries between the Ptolemies and Bonaparte the surrounding streets had risen to this level and the fifty-foot height of the temple itself was completely filled with sand rubble. After it had been disinterred Mehemet Ali thought it would make a good gunpowder store; fortunately he was dissuaded.

The temple is a creation entirely of Ptolemaic and Roman times and from beginning to end its building and decoration covered nearly four hundred years. The Ptolemies who began it are represented perhaps naturally in the guise of Ancient Egyptian Pharaohs, but those who are familiar with the sculpture of ancient Rome will gaze with astonishment at the portrayal of its emperors. Here, amongst others, we see Domitian encountering an Egyptian deity; Trajan dressed as a Pharaoh in the process of slaughtering his enemies; and even more surprisingly, since he may have seen it with his own eyes, the Emperor Septimius Severus similarly got up and followed by his Egyptianised family. After one of his sons, Geta, had been murdered by his other son, Caracalla, the Egyptian priests did not omit their duty of erasing Geta from this family group.

What survives of the temple, and in almost perfect preservation, is the Hypostyle Hall of three curtain walls and twenty-four

columns. The attention is arrested immediately by the capitals of
the columns, no longer the solemn heavy papyrus bud or 'umble'
capitals of Ancient Egypt but a series of elaborately carved arrangements in the shapes of plants and foliage, in no less than sixteen
different designs. By comparison with the traditional columns of
Ancient Egypt, this is indeed a human moment; the humanity
becomes even more appealing when one sees sculpted in stone on
top of some of the leaves of the capitals the figures of two innocent-
looking frogs. The usual expanses of incised and raised reliefs
cover both walls and columns; some of the raised reliefs on the
walls are arranged in successive tiers of pleasing rectangles; elsewhere and on the columns other designs and hieroglyphics take
over—hieroglyphics, the Egyptologists tell us, of really deplorable
quality. But at Esna we are nearing the end of an Age; these are
probably in date the latest decorations and inscriptions that have
survived from the traditional work of Ancient Egypt.

Edfu, which is our next stage, is a grander affair than Esna. It is
commonly described as the most perfect of Egyptian temples. Built
entirely in the Ptolemaic era, it was clearly designed to a specific
plan which was not altered in the building. It is also unique among
Egyptian temples in being virtually complete; this, in spite of the
fact that, like Esna, it was situated in the middle of a town and
until excavated by Mariette in 1860 was buried up to the level of
its capitals. Many of its reliefs, sadly, were mutilated in Christian
times; but architecturally speaking, it is virtually intact.

The temple impresses not only by its design but also by its
proportions. A grand first pylon gives entrance to a great forecourt,
surrounded by columns, twelve on each of its long sides, six and
eight at the two ends. Much trouble was taken with the capitals,
which are of the floral type. On the long sides no two capitals are
the same but each capital matches its opposite number on the other
side. The most prominent object in the forecourt is the famous
falcon-headed statue of Horus, the god to whom apparently the
temple was dedicated.

A second pylon leads to the first Hypostyle Hall. This is an
affair of eighteen columns, again with good capitals, and of two
contrasting decorative styles. On the columns and on the near
wall are reliefs of the incised type, while the two end walls are
beautifully done with raised reliefs. What impresses one here as at
Esna is that the decorative scheme was planned as a whole and a
satisfying sense of symmetry results. This makes a striking contrast
to the temples of the older Egypt in which, though every square

foot may be sculpted, the impression too often is of a gigantic hotchpotch with bits and pieces added haphazardly or as after-thoughts in order to fill the available space.

The sense of symmetry continues through the remaining sections of the temple, the next one being the second Hypostyle Hall of twelve columns. Beyond it, through two further halls, one penetrates to the sanctuary where an unexpected object confronts one—an enormous empty granite shrine—placed here apparently as an after-thought for it is of the period of Nectanebis, a Pharaoh some fifty years anterior to the temple's foundation.

The temple, finally, is interesting in having preserved completely its ambulatory and surrounding wall. These are no less minutely and exhaustively sculptured than the interior halls. An interesting diversion on the eastern side is to dive down the steps to the Nilometer, one of the few surviving in Egypt from ancient times. For the athletic a more exciting diversion is to climb the 242 steps to the top of the Pylon; the view from the top is unusually attractive, embracing not only the temple in all its details but a wide panorama of the Nile Valley with its villages and palm trees and in the distance on each side the cliffs which mark the desert sky line. Not the least of the charms of the Edfu are the horse-carriages which transport the visitor between the temple and the ship.

The last temple before Assuan is Kom Ombo. This is another Ptolemaic temple like Edfu, though smaller and less well preserved; but of all Egyptian temples it has a unique charm. This is due to its situation on a lofty knoll half encircled by a bend of the Nile which gives the effect of a sort of acropolis against the background of cultivation, desert skyline and blue sky. The temple, further, is interesting in being dedicated not to one, but to two gods, Sobek (or Souchos) and Haroeris. Architecturally the result is singular; the temple forms a perfect and symmetrical whole but the openings and the chambers are so disposed as to form two separate entities divided from each other, so to speak, by an invisible line, the north side being Haroeris and the south Sobek.

The builders were too ambitious, or too trusting of the river; some of the building has been undermined and the north (Haroeris) side of the entrance pylon has subsided. Once again the Roman Emperors figure prominently; Tiberius is much displayed upon the outer walls; on the south side of the pylon, which has survived, we see Domitian making presentations to the local gods. Not much of the courtyard survives, but we may see the lower portions of the sixteen columns with which it was once adorned where once more Tiberius is much in evidence. The Vestibule or first Hypostyle Hall has more to show; here survive ten columns with rich floral and palm capitals and a variety of sunk-reliefs and bas-reliefs dating from Ptolemaic times; notice also the astronomical scenes on the underside of the roof. The main or second Hypostyle Hall which follows is smaller; beyond are openings which lead to the twin sanctuaries of the two gods in whose honour the temple was built. Before leaving Kom Ombo it should be mentioned that Sobek was the god of the crocodiles once prolific in this area but now extinct; in a small unfinished chapel of Hathor there remain a number of their mummified corpses.

Assuan, which is the next (and final) stop on the boat trip, is the second landmark for the traveller in Upper Egypt for here again is a town which is in some degree adapted for the residence of the Western traveller. Without the outstanding interest which Karnak and Thebes give to Luxor, Assuan is by no means devoid of interest for the sightseer. Scenically it is much more beautiful and as such it also has achieved a world-wide fame as a winter-resort; its scenic quality can be judged from the fact that the late Aga Khan, who had all the world to choose from, chose Assuan as his last resting-place and as the site of his tomb.

The *raison d'être* of the town is the First Cataract. This is the name given to the rapids which here descend the Nile and which obstruct the navigation of anything except small boats. The effect of the fall of the river has been to divide the channel and to create through a course of several miles a number of isolated rocks and of islands large and small. It is the first of these islands that is overlooked by the town.

The town, like Luxor, is on the right bank and in shape and layout is not dissimilar. An agreeable corniche follows the river side. At the southern end the level rises and here has been built the celebrated Cataract Hotel, now supplemented by the New Cataract. The town, again like Luxor, is not of a size to have an extensive bazaar or souk, but on the inland streets parallel to the river there are a number of shops and plenty of scope for bargaining. For those whose zest for sightseeing is insatiable there is in the town itself, not far from the Cataract Hotel, a small and agreeable Ptolemaic temple.

Opposite the town is the considerable island of Elephantine, so called, it is said, from the fact that it was here in ancient times that was first encountered the African elephant. It is also thought that this was the site of the earliest town. Elephantine is now a beauty spot largely covered with trees and gardens, but preserving at its southern end a number of objects for the sightseer. The first of these is a small museum, inconsiderable by comparison with the other Egyptian museums of the world but interesting from the fact that its contents are of specifically local provenance. Close to it is another of Egypt's famous Nilometers, this one ninety steps deep and bearing interesting records of the flood levels of past ages. Close to it also is the site of what once must have been a major temple dedicated to the god Khnoum. The northern portion of the island has been appropriated for the ultra-modern and very grand Oberoi Hotel. Though the building can claim to be an ornament in itself, the fact of its construction clearly throws a question mark over the future development of the island and poses some challenge to the planning authorities of Assuan.

Between Elephantine and the west bank is Kitchener island, once the property of Lord Kitchener and now of the Egyptian government. It is a small island planted with trees and completely laid out as a botanic garden; a charming and welcome refuge from the heat, noise, smells and the other appurtenances of Egyptian travel.

Assuan has also a number of interesting excursions on its opposite (or west) bank beyond the islands. Here, for those whose sightseeing appetite is still not satisfied, is another extensive tomb-area designed apparently for local princes who ruled here during the later dynasties of the Old Kingdom. Of particular interest to Egyptologists has been the tomb of Hirkhouf for it is inscribed with a long and elaborate account of four expeditions made by the deceased as caravan-conductor to four different parts of Central Africa. For the ordinary visitor the most rewarding tombs are those of Sirenpont I and Sirenpont II, both of the Twelfth-Dynasty period and both with interesting decorations.

Much more prominent in the view is the cupola surmounting the rectangular building which is the mausoleum of the Aga Khan. This has been built since the Aga Khan's death in 1957; his body reposes in a fine white marble sarcophagus adorned with inscriptions from the Koran. Close to it has been built the attractive house and garden which provides a winter residence for his widow the Begum.

A very different excursion is to the monastry of St Simeon some twenty minutes further on. This is one of Egypt's oldest and best surivivals of a Coptic monastery, built probably in the seventh century AD; notwithstanding that it has been deserted certainly since the thirteenth century, it is astonishingly well preserved. A wall some twenty feet high surrounds it; inside are buildings, some of which are preserved to the upper floor. Chief among them is the large monastery church which has, alas, lost the two domes of its name, though part of the apse survives with its semi-domes. It is interesting to climb the steps and view the upper storey with a central corridor and the monks' sleeping quarters and later to try to identify the ancillary buildings in the main courtyard such as store-rooms, bakehouse and bath.

Part of the interest of the Assuan district is that it was from here that came a large part of the building material of Ancient Egypt. In the Western Desert beyond the monastery is a sandstone quarry still containing part of an obelisk with an inscription of Seti I; and to the north of Assuan is the so-called Alabaster Hill from which the Ancient Egyptians mined quartz. The main quarries from which the Egyptians obtained the granite which features so largely in their obelisks and statues are about one and half miles south of the town. In the southern quarry may be seen unfinished sarcophagi, an unfinished colossus of a Pharaoh and a statue of Osiris; more usually shown to tourists is the northern quarry where there still lies an enormous obelisk completely quarried but never removed.

Not the least of the charms of Assuan are the boat trips necessary for some of the excursions. The Egyptian felucca, with its white sail so suggestive of a swallow's wing, has an infinite capacity for slowness, but there are a few pleasanter ways of idling away a sunny afternoon. The modern tourist is seldom invited to sample the rapids, but it is possible to go as far as the island of Sihel, interesting to antiquarians on account of the enormous number of ancient inscriptions still visible on its rocks.

In the nineteenth century the favourite excursion was to the island of Philae, one of the islands in the rapids some five miles south of the town. Alas, that modern engineering has intervened. Under the British occupation the decision was taken to build downstream from Philae the Assuan dam, the first major effort in the long-drawn-out battles to control the inundations of the Nile. The first dam completed in 1898 was raised in 1912 and was raised again in 1933. The sad consequence for the tourist was that for most of the year the islands above it were submerged. The famous vegetation of Philae was destroyed and during the few months when the buildings were visible they emerged covered with the slime deposited by the Nile. The construction of the new Nasser dam upstream from Philae is thought to have brought more pressing dangers. In the face of this the brave decision has been taken to remove the buildings to a new site and re-erect them on another island some three hundred yards away and permanently above flood level. So ambitious a project might be thought to belong to the world of fantasy until we see what has actually been achieved at Abu Simbel. In the meantime, alas, and until the re-erection is completed, Philae is off the tourist list and one can only write of the Philae that once was.

Herodotus, though he visited Elephantine, does not mention Philae and the evidence of the surviving buildings suggests that the island did not begin to be developed until shortly after his visit. Nectanebis of the Thirteenth Dynasty is the earliest Pharaoh whose buildings now survive and it was extensively built on by the Ptolemies. The Roman emperors evidently appreciated its charms: Claudius built a small temple, Trajan the famous kiosk and Hadrian the gateway which still survives. Astonishingly the worship of Ancient Egypt which had been prohibited by the Edict of Theodosius in AD 383 here survived and it was not until the Byzantine emperor Justinian sent an armed force to the island about AD 535 that the temple of Isis finally became a Christian church. When Europeans discovered it, some of its buildings were still in place and the beauty of the island was such that it became known as the Pearl of Egypt. Robert Curzon, who visited the island three times in the 1820s and 1830s, thus describes his impressions: 'The scenery around consists of an infinity of steep granite rocks which stand, some in the water, others on the land, all of them of the wildest and most picturesque forms.... The sacred island of Philae, the burial-place of Osiris, is covered with buildings, temples, colonnades, gateways and terrace-walks, which are magnificent even in their ruin.... The silence and solemn grandeur of the immense buildings around me were most imposing; and on emerging from the lofty gateway between the two towers of the propylon...the tufts of palms which are here of great height with their weeping branches seem to be mourning over the desolation....'

One surprising historical record on Philae is a French inscription of 1798 that Desaix arrived as far as here in his pursuit of his elusive Mameluke; harder to believe is the fact that in the subsequent thirty years there was abstracted from here, with the primitive resources then available, the Ptolemaic obelisk which has since graced the garden of Kingston Lacy.

A description of Philae can be thus only from the printed descriptions of what it once was, fortified by the hope that it may be again. The island is about 500 yards long by about 160 yards broad. It was the seat of the worship of the goddess Isis and at one time was almost entirely built over. The oldest surviving building, the temple of Nectanebis, was at the south-west corner immediately above the river. From it there led a colonnade to the great temple of Isis, a colonnade which is described as being one of the most attractive features of the island. Much the greatest building was the temple of Isis itself. This was begun by Ptolemy II Philadelphus and finished by his successor, Ptolemy III Evergetes, both of whom resigned in the third century before Christ. It was a building on a considerable scale and in the traditional Egyptian pattern; the entrance pylon was 150 feet across and 60 feet in height; and the pylon towers were adorned with reliefs, some con-temporary with the building and some added at later times. There followed the usual forecourt and the Birth House. The temple had a second pylon and a sanctuary and the customary store rooms, but apparently no hypostyle hall. To the west of the second pylon was Hadrian's gateway and north of this was the chapel of Osiris with reliefs of the Roman emperors Augustus and Tiberius. The so-called Kiosk, the symbol of the island and built by the emperor Trajan, was on the eastern side.

From the lost world of Philae it is an abrupt transition to be brought face to face with the new Nasser dam. This gigantic enter-prise, as we have already noted, has been intimately involved with some of the most painful vicissitudes of Egypt in the mid-twentieth century. It was 1955 before the plans were initiated, 1960 before the works began, 1964 before the Nile waters were first harnessed, 1972 before the work was completed. Three hundred workmen lost their lives in the undertaking, thirty thousand spectators attended the formal opening.

The barrage was so sited as to create a water reserve infinitely larger than anything comtemplated by the original Assuan dam. The lake which it has created is on such a scale that it covers also a large area in the Sudan south of the Egyptian border; its total length is something like three hundred miles with an average width of some six miles; an entire population has been displaced by the enterprise. For those who like statistics, the dimensions of the barrage itself are sufficiently impressive: base a thousand yards wide, summit fifty yards wide, height more than a hundred yards, length over two miles; the total volume of the material used is estimated to be about six times that of the Great Pyramid.

While there are doubts about the reason for the Great Pyramid, there are no doubts about the reason for the new Nasser dam; it derives from the remorseless demands of demography. Egypt depends utterly on its cultivable land; the population during the years that the dam was building was increasing at the rate of nearly one million per year; in one generation, from 1945 to 1975, the population doubled from eighteen to thirty-six million. For Nasser the undertaking of this project became a matter of desperate urgency. Clearly beyond the financial and technical resources of Egypt itself, the project was first entrusted to the western world; fate intervened and by an abrupt reversal the whole enterprise was confided to the Soviet Union. What we see today is the triumph of Russian technology.

One of the least important results of the project was that it would put an end to all sightseeing upstream from the new barrage. A desperate attempt was made to identify and rescue everything that was about to be submerged. Fourteen temples or monuments were selected which it was thought deserved to be preserved; the aid of UNESCO was invoked; hasty excavations and dismantlings followed; some temples were removed and rebuilt; others were put in packing cases awaiting a site where they could start a new life. By a singular reversion to the times of Mehemet Ali a series of presentations were made to friendly foreign countries; one gift was made to Turin and three temples were presented respectively to Spain, the Netherlands and the USA. There remained the greatest challenge, Abu Simbel.

Abu Simbel is an astonishing experience for three separate reasons; first, its remoteness; secondly, its size; and thirdly, the scale of the operation which has been undertaken to preserve it. It is about one hundred and seventy miles south of Assuan and though other temples and ancient settlements clearly intervened along the river valley it seems astounding that so colossal an enterprise should have been undertaken in the remote heart of Africa. Though the techniques of Abu Simbel are the same as those we have seen in countless tombs, its two great temples are unique in not being built above ground, but created by enormous excavations in the sandstone rock.

'The two rock temples of Abu Simbel,' wrote James Baikie in 1932, 'of which the larger is the greatest and finest piece of work of its kind which was ever accomplished by an Egyptian architect, are hewn out of the face of two sandstone cliffs which come down to the bank of the river.... When Belzoni saw them at his first visit, the Great Temple was so far buried in the sand that the head of only one of the colossi appeared above the drift.... M. Barsanti has done what can be done to protect the temple against being overwhelmed once more beneath the ceaseless flow of the sand... but it is to be feared that man will here, as elsewhere, wage a fruitless battle in the end against nature and that the great temple will finally be buried. That completion of its destiny will not come, however, until man has ceased to value one of the greatest works of the past sufficiently to consider it worth protecting.'

How different, since Baikie wrote, has been the destiny of the great temple! With the decision to build the new Nasser dam it became apparent that the whole monument would become permanently submerged beneath the new lake. A world-wide appeal was launched; international co-operation was achieved upon an unheard scale; finally UNESCO stepped into the breach and undertook responsibility for the greatest work of architectural salvage the world has ever seen.

Both the great and the smaller temple were saved. The scale of the operation may be judged by the fact that apart from the four huge colossi which adorn the exterior, the great temple was an excavated building, driven 180 feet into the living rock. The decision was taken to move both temples two hundred yards westwards, raising them at the same time to positions some two hundred feet higher than the original. The Blue Guide of 1975 describes the six stages of the operation. First, it was necessary, without using explosives, to remove the cliffs which surmounted the temple façades — a hundred feet in the case of the great temple — and with other excavation to remove about 300,000 tons of rock. Simultaneously — for the work was being carried out against time — a huge coffer dam had to be built to keep out the rising waters. Thirdly, the temples had to be cut out of the rock by sawing; 1,036 separate blocks were cut out, some of them weighing up to thirty tons. They then had to be numbered and transported. Fifthly, and this was the most difficult stage, the blocks had to be remounted by affixing them to a superstructure of concrete, while maintaining their respective positions and orientations. Finally came the reconstruction, as faithfully as possible, on the original plan by the erection of concrete vaults sufficient to support an overlay of rock similar to the original cliff sides. The whole operation took nine years and involved nine hundred workers.

Both temples date from the time of Rameses II. The smaller

temple is dedicated to the favourite cow-goddess Hathor and but for the proximity of the great temple, this temple itself would have been a wonder of the world. It is fronted by six colossi carved in the sandstone on each side of the entrance portal, including two of Rameses and one of his wife Nefertari, and carved royal children cluster round their feet. The interior chambers consist of Forecourt or Hypostyle Hall, Vestibule and Sanctuary, all of which are decorated with reliefs. Space has been allotted to Nefertari, but in the main the scenes are a glorification of Rameses usually in conjunction with one or more of the familiar gods.

The great temple is dedicated to the three gods Amun, Ptah and Harakte, and has a façade 119 feet wide and about 100 feet high. The first view of it is one of the most impressive things in Egypt for it is fronted by four colossal statues—not of the three gods but of Rameses himself—hewn out of rock and about sixty five feet high, that is about the same size as the two colossi of Memnon which we have seen at Thebes. But the Abu Simbel statues are infinitely better preserved; apart from some damage to the nearest left-hand statue the carving is virtually perfect and astonishingly it does not appear to have been eroded by blown sand. Once again the royal children in sandstone are grouped around the legs. The interior chambers here are on a much more extensive scale; there is a large Hypostyle Hall and a Small Hypostyle Hall before the Antechamber and the Sanctuary. God-like figures representing Rameses, some with the crown of Upper Egypt others with the double crown and themselves some thirty feet in height, front the dividing pillars of the first hall; notice also the well preserved painted decoration on the ceiling of nave and aisles. The reliefs on the walls are more spirited than those in the small temple but they are not more original; they represent the favourite life scenes of Rameses and inevitably his battle with the Hittites. The second hall and the vestibule are more religious; Rameses makes offerings to gods, and his queen participates. The Sanctuary still has the broken support for the sacred boat standing in the middle of the floor.

Having seen the antiquities one may graduate to a very different style of sightseeing. Behind the temple and within the framework of the new mountain is the concrete dome by which it is all supported. It is an astonishing experience to climb up the modern stairs and admire the new technology. Perhaps after all the crimes and destructions of our age this construction may survive as a reminder that not all was crime and destruction in the twentieth century.

11 PRESENT AND FUTURE

From the terrace of the new Abu Simbel we gaze out upon the latest portent of the new Egypt, Lake Nasser. We have already noticed the demographic compulsions which drove Egypt's rulers to project this gradiose scheme. But while aware of its physical scale we have hardly appreciated its dimensions. The Nasser dam and Lake Nasser have as their avowed objective the controlling and the regulating of the entire economic life of Egypt, something no country in history has done before.

Until Mehemet Ali Egypt lived almost entirely by agriculture. After Mehemet Ali it was still agriculture, but with the difference that the new cotton cultivation provided opportunity for a profitable export trade. In later times great efforts have been made to break out of this traditional mould, but the resources have been lacking. Egypt has no great coal-fields, no great oil-fields, no mountains to produce cheap electrical energy; and in consequence Egypt has had little industrial expertise. The Suez Canal was a minor break-out but the wealth of Egypt in international terms remained commercial and not industrial — the Suez Canal, cotton and whatever agricultural surplus could be exported. The prime consideration — for the population had to be fed — was still agriculture.

We have described the Egyptian agriculture of ancient tradition, the extraordinary annual sequence of inundation, sowing and harvest. It was a single crop economy and it was essentially hit-and-miss for everything depended upon the behaviour of the Nile. If it failed to rain in Abyssinia, Egypt starved. If it rained too much in Abyssinia, the country would be half ruined. In every season, high or low, vast masses of Nile water poured away uselessly into the Mediterranean. To regulate this annual flood, to substitute certainty for hit-and-miss, to be able to know the times of ebb and flow and to have some assurance of the water volume seemed a self-evident goal for the thinking ruler. And yet the advantages of the old haphazard system were not negligible. The occasional floods cleansed the entire country. The surplus waters helped in the Delta to maintain the water table. The Mediterranean around the Delta coast was a sea almost of fresh water. Above all, the annual inundation brought its annual incalculable gift, the silt deposit which was at once the raw material and the fertiliser of the all-important soil.

Much of this was altered by the old Assuan dam. The occasional destructive flood was eliminated. The annual flood was so regulated that the arable countryside was no longer inundated. Irrigation was maintained through the seasons in such a way that the soil could be permanently productive. Egypt became a country of two or three annual crops. The surplus discharge into the Mediterranean was greatly reduced. The agricultural output was greatly increased.

The Nasser dam is an effort to produce a major expansion on what has already been achieved. The first objective is to irrigate and fertilise and bring into production large areas which hitherto for lack of water have never produced at all. A second objective is to perfect the irrigation system over the already productive areas. A third is to supply the country with what must be the first necessity in the modern world for any country with industrial ambitions, an abundant source of energy. This last objective has been achieved by the incorporation in the Nasser dam of a gigantic hydro-electric complex involving twelve turbines. And it has produced its first results in industrialisation—a steel works at Helouan and a large factory for making aluminium from imported bauxite. Minor objectives have been the rendering of the navigation of the Nile practicable at all seasons and a pronounced increase in the regular production of one of the all-important agricultural resources of Egypt, the rice crop.

For the projectors of so colossal an untertaking the doubts must have resided in the fears of the unknowable and unknown. The prophets of doom have not been lacking. The chief beneficiary would not be Egypt but the Sudan, which from its geographical position has been able to bargain for a very substantial proportion of the irrigation waters. The loss from evaporation would be enormous and still more dangerous would be the seepage into the subsoil. The climate of Upper Egypt would be transformed. Sixty thousand peasants would have to be evacuated from the flooded area and given land elsewhere. The water level of the Delta would be lowered. Salinity would invade the soil from the Mediterranean, whose salinity would itself be affected. The occasional healthful cleansing of the country by high floods would cease. The incidence of the dreaded bilharzia would certainly increase. Above all, the annual silt deposit on which the soil of Egypt had depended for millennia would finally be lost and the silt itself would accumulate uselessly behind the dam, gradually filling the lake.

In the few years that have elapsed since the lake became a working project it may be said that on the whole the evil prophecies have not materialised. The Sudan did indeed strike a hard bargain. The 60,000 peasants had indeed to be displaced and re-settled. There was indeed a very noticeable seepage in the years when the lake gradually filled. Up to the year 1971 the annual inflows were generous and the lake expanded; as new ground was first covered, the seepage was too evident. Then in 1972 and 1973 came two years of low flood; the lake area actually decreased but the seepage also decreased dramatically. Further years of high flood materialised and though the seepage was still evident the lake did in fact completely fill. Evaporation there obviously was, but not on the scale the pessimists had predicted nor was the local climate appreciably changed.

What effect the new project has had on the bilharzia problem it is too early to say. This is the scourge which, transmitted through organisms in the Nile water, has for countless centuries infected the Egyptian peasant. The cure for it must surely lie, not in the sphere of water flow but in purified drinking water and in efficient and up-to-date medication. Nor has it yet been possible completely to analyse the effects on the soil and subsoil of the Delta. What has resulted, and what had already resulted from the original Assuan dam was the need to replace the life-giving silt with artificial fertilisers; fortunately for Egypt these have been found within the national boundaries and henceforward they will play the vital part in the national production.

The most depressing estimate made as a consequence of the new scheme is that in five hundred years the lake will be completely filled with silt. In any country except Egypt this would seem an incredibly distant perspective; seen against the background of the millennia of Egyptian history it appears a trivial interval of time. The consolation must be that surely within this period modern human ingenuity will have invented a means whereby the problem can be tackled.

One of the more bizarre consequences of the project is said to be that sharks are now being attracted from the Red Sea through the Suez Canal into the Mediterranean. This is the result of the increased salinity of the sea water as compared with the days when the Nile overflow kept it permanently brackish or half-fresh. But the consequences may be less serious for the Egyptians than for the frequenters of Monte Carlo and St Tropez.

In spite of what are obviously the tremendous potential achievements of the project, two major questions must continue to overhang it. First, is it secure? Secondly, can it succeed?

As to its security. The project is the greatest exercise in the sphere of river control that the world has seen. But the spine-chilling thought remains: Egypt does not in fact control its own river. Only for the last few hundred miles of its course does the Nile flow through Egyptian territory. The White Nile, which provides the steady flow, originates in the republics of Zaire, Tanzania, Kenya, Uganda. The Blue Nile, which provides the annual flood, originates in Ethiopia. The rivers unite at Khartoum in the Sudan and it is through the republic of the Sudan that the Nile flows for the greater part of its course. The mere construction of Lake Nasser—which has flooded part of their country—must have opened the eyes of the Sudanese to what can be done with a river. Already the Russians who, after building the Nasser dam, were unceremoniously turned out of Egypt, are rumoured to be planning with the Ethiopians a series of dams on the Blue Nile which could deprive Egypt (and the Sudan) of one-third of the river flow. None of this can be pleasant thinking for the present rulers of Egypt.

As to whether it can succeed. To suggest such doubts is not to criticise the vision or the achievement of the project itself. It is simply to face and recognise the enormity of the problems of modern Egypt. We have described the scheme as the logical consequence of the pressures of demography. But the grim fact remains that the demographic pressures, so far from disappearing as a result of this great solution, show every sign of increasing until they become insoluble. The population, which in 1900 was ten million, is now forty million, it increases every year by one million, by the end of the century it will be sixty million. In 1973, for the first time in history, Egypt, which in ancient times was the granary of the Mediterranean world, ceased to be able to feed its own population; by the end of the present decade Egypt is expected to have become the largest wheat-importing country in the world.

Against these remorseless trends can the benefits of the Nasser dam prevail? The reclamation of newly irrigated areas for agriculture; the duplication of crops; the provision of new employment opportunities in industry—will these achievements even begin to keep up with the remorseless population growth? Or will some spectacular new initiative be needed if the country is to survive?

One such spectacular initiative is already under consideration. We have in this study of Egypt said little about the desert areas, covering though they do some 90% of the country. West of Cairo in the Libyan desert is the Katara depression, an enormous desert area many feet below the Mediterranean level. A canal or vast pipe line to take the Mediterranean waters into the depression suggests exciting possibilities. It could result in the production of enormous quantities of electric power. It might make possible the reclamation of present desert areas for agriculture. It might alter the desert climate. It might provide a vast new scope for a fishery. The salt deposited might provide the raw material for a variety of chemical industries.

The question then remains: has Egypt the resources for such a project? It is possible that the technical expertise could be found within the country; what is certain is that, as in the case of the Nasser dam, the financial resources are lacking. Which brings one back to the central problem of Egypt's economic state.

For years past the country has been bankrupt. Burdened with gigantic foreign debts, Egypt has been successively in pawn to the Soviet Union, the International Monetary Fund, the oil-rich countries of the Arab world and the United States of America. The interest on such debts, or even such part of it as is paid, is an appalling burden upon the country and its inhabitants. Only by building up a favourable trade balance could there be any hope of discharging such liabilities—and the indications at present are all the other way. To undertake a project like Katara the country would be thrown back once again on foreign financial aid.

Next to the burden of foreign debts the country's greatest burden has been its armaments. A formidable proportion of the national income has for years past been spent on arms and much of it has had to be in foreign currency. Anything that could relieve this burden would be a major benefit for the country. And this is coming to be realised, and with it the realisation that the only prescription for reducing the armaments burden is peace. Since Israel proclaimed its national identity in 1948, there have been four Israeli wars, 1948, 1956, 1967 and 1973. All four wars taxed the country's resources, but the major problem has been sustaining financially the high level of armaments that has had to be kept in being during all this time.

But it is necessary to personalise the problems. The young Egyptian of today, if born in the city, grows up in the appalling environment we shall shortly describe; if born in the country, in the mud brick village of the Egyptian vernacular. Both in town and country he is probably conscripted for service in the army. Life in the Egyptian army is certainly no luxury, but the army provides certain standards and it may teach him a trade. From the army the town boy returns to the rat-race of Alexandria or Cairo. The country boy may wish to return to the family fields. But in the country the population pressure is constant; already in the last century the amount of land available to each individual peasant has been enormously reduced and the process remorselessly continues. Equipped with his army-taught skills he arrives in Cairo to seek a job and finds himself condemned to exist in a shack among the gigantic shanty towns that crowd the suburbs of a city where nothing seems to work, where the man-holes heave from the pressure of escaping sewer gas and where even in a car it can take two hours to do ten miles. A recent visitor thus describes the Cairo scene: 'A fair proportion of the population live in miniscule hovels or rudimentary tents in a setting that defies description: miles and miles of apparent devastation that resembles the immediate aftermath of an earthquake; adults and children toil, like ants, up and down mountains of rubble; going where it is difficult to imagine. ...Where there are colonies of flats built among the rubble, the effect is of the aftermath of bombing raids. The houses are falling down or simply have not been finished. The builders have run out, not of money but of materials like wood and cement, because the government cannot afford to import these things.'

If our young Egyptian is a lad of enterprise the solution is to emigrate. And there has in fact in the past few years been a large emigration with results that are both bad and good; on the bad side Egypt has lost a lot of her best brains; on the good side the financial remittances made by the emigrants to their families have become so large as to make a substantial contribution to the Egyptian economy.

There is not much profit in raking over the recent Egyptian past. Opinions will long differ regarding the regime of Nasser (still worshipped by his countrymen) and the balance of benefit or hardship that he brought to the New Egypt; but the probable verdict must be that he had much to answer for. In the 1970s Egypt found herself with a ruler of a new type, a ruler of vision, logical decision and astonishing political courage. The measures taken by President Sadat within a decade would be unbelievable if they were not true. In 1972, when the country was largely dependent on Russian arms and Russian technology, he took the decision to dismiss 20,000

Russian technicians and turn them out of the country. In 1973, in face of the precedent of three previous disastrous wars, he launched his country on a fourth war with Israel and brought Egypt through it, if not as victor, at any rate as a country which had fought the Israelis to an honourable draw and had greatly enhanced its military reputation. In 1975, in face of all the risks involved—for no peace had been declared—he decreed the re-opening of the Suez Canal and secured for Egypt the great financial benefits that this could earn. From 1975 onwards, though this was done much more quietly, he began to reverse the policy of universal national-isation which had been Nasser's guiding star and openly to encourage the foreign investment which had suffered such dis-illusionment under his predecessor's regime. Symbolically the old Cairo bourse began to be redecorated in anticipation of the day when share dealings would again become the norm of Egyptian business. In 1976 he formally abrogated the Russo-Egyptian treaty. Finally in 1977 he took the momentous decision to begin to seek peace with Israel.

All these decisions involved great risks; but it is difficult to exaggerate the risks entailed in the latest decision. Ever since 1948, when the Arab world had first been outraged by the proclamation of the State of Israel, Egypt had been the centre of Arab resistance, the seat and centre of the Arab League which formalised the hostility of the Arab world. She had, as we have seen, four times fought against the State of Israel with more or less help from other Arab countries. For many years—for Egypt was initially the richest of the Arab countries—she had provided most of the sinews of war and resistance. By the 1970s, thanks to the transformation brought about by the oil discoveries, the situation was dramatically changed; Egypt was now one of the poorest of the Arab states; poor to the extent that she was becoming financially dependent upon some of her richer Arab allies.

If Egypt is now to be officially at peace with Israel there is little reason to hope that all other Arab countries will follow suit. The saddest political phenomenon of the modern world is the political fragmentation of Arabia, a state of affairs not like to be remedied in our own age. Some of the Arab countries will not merely refuse to be at peace with Israel, there is reason to fear they will wreak their wrath on Egypt. For Egypt's ruler the threat is personal as well as political; for the rest of his life he must walk under the shadow of the fear of assassination. On the political plane it is easy for those who have never visited Palestine, who have never seen the refugee camps, to lambast the intransigeance of the Arab world. But if Egypt is to be at peace with Israel, it means surrendering—on her part—three causes which have been most vividly at the heart of Arab resistance: the return of the refugees to their homes, the return of the West Bank and the Gaza strip to Arab rule, and the integrity of the Holy Places. The first cause affects particularly the Kingdom of Jordan, the second both Jordan and Egypt, the third perhaps deserves a less summary treatment for its affects particularly the Arab Kingdom which must be a key factor in any future developments in the Arab world, Saudi Arabia.

The Holy Places of Islam are primarily Mecca, Medina and Jerusalem. Mecca and Medina are within the territory and under the protection of Saudi Arabia. In Jerusalem, whereas the New City has been Israeli-ruled since 1948, the Old City was until the 1967 war part of the territory of Jordan and so under Arab rule. Sacred also to the Jews and the Christians, the Old City contains not only the famous Dome of the Rock from which Mohammed made his ascent to heaven but also the Mosque of El-Aksa which next to Mecca and Medina is the most sacred place of Islam. The Arab world in general and the Saudi rulers in particular have never reconciled themselves to the incorporation of these religious monuments in the State of Israel. Time was when Saudi Arabia, poor, primitive and remote, could be forgotten or ignored. Since the vast development of its oil-rich territories the position is fantastically altered. Now a hostile Saudi Arabia, accessible, powerful and rich beyond imagination, could be a dangerous enemy to Egypt.

The Egyptian leader now finds himself trapped, both externally and internally, between pressures which to all appearances are irreconcilable. Externally, he faces the prospect of the indefinite hostility of many or most of the Arab countries who should be his allies. He can only terminate this by breaking with the country that has at last become his great support, the United States of America. Sadat's recent treaty-making initiatives are the expression of his proclaimed political philosophy: 'The United States holds 99% of the cards in the Middle East.' Let us hope his assessment is correct.

To the poor poverty-stricken Cairene amidst his shacks and rubbish heaps, to the equally poverty-stricken fellah working all day his miserable patch under the Egyptian sun, these external pressures between which his ruler lives may appear considerations that are impossibly remote. Far different is it with the internal pressures, for these directly affect the living standards of every Egyptian, urban and rural alike. Internally, Egypt's ruler constantly faces the pressure of the national creditors who threaten to refuse all further aid unless the national budget is balanced. But to balance the budget means primarily to abolish or drastically reduce the government subsidies paid to keep the cost of living at anything like a reasonable level. In 1977, under the creditors' pressure it was announced that the subsidies would be cut. The result was an explosion, a vast reaction of rioting which it was feared at one stage would equal the riots of 1952 and similarly topple the regime. The regime survived but the answer was clear; subsidies could not be cut; hence, among other consequences, the builders who have to stop work because there is no more cement or wood.

The regime survived, but in the modern Arab world almost any regime is permanently at risk. Yet it is pertinent to enquire from whence the risk might come, from what section of society is there the will, the organisation or the resources for a political démarche. In Egypt the present answer must be, the army; it was the army which organised the expulsion of the last monarch and inaugurated the New Egypt of Nasser; it is only the army which contains the potential will and ability once more to transform the political scene. But the sad truth is that even if a new regime was instituted, the problems it would face would not be new; the old problems would remain.

In this brief assessment we have circled round, without confronting, the two greatest problems of all, population and religion. In so doing, we are, so far as population is concerned, only imitating what the Egyptian rulers themselves have done. Two modern statistics give the dimensions of the challenge; the death rate of 13% compares with a birth rate of 35%; of the existing population 42% is aged under 14 years. Contraceptives have in fact been on sale in Egypt since 1955; in 1965 a Supreme Council for Family Planning was instituted. But at no time has there been any effective lead from above. All tradition is against it; bureaucratic inefficiency does the rest. Yet the prospect is so self-evident that sooner or later it must be faced up to; a major effort of national will is called for; it is not too much to say that the future of the Egyptian race may depend upon its willingness to forego its own procreation.

So far as religion is concerned, an intelligent projection is much more difficult. On the limited question of population control, European countries have in the past years run into objections from the Roman Catholic Church. What is the attitude of Islam? So far there has been a deafening silence. But Islam is not a religion which is renowned for its obeisance to logic, and certainly not to economic logic. On the wider and general plane, what is Egypt's religious future and what influence will religion have in its future problems? The important fact which we have already noticed is that Islam has awoken from the torpor of centuries and is now once again a religion on the march. In its first hundred years it physically conquered half the known world; today, physical conquest is out of fashion but what spiritual and mental conquests may lie in store? The religion is indeed on the march but it is too early to forecast its destination; one can only say that both for the world and for Egypt the consequences could be momentous.

While a religious solution may be found, we have in this chapter reached the point of writing off Egypt as a country to which there is no economic solution. But, curiously, problems have a strange way, in the long run, of solving themselves even when it has been irrefutably proved by statisticians and economists that there can be no solution. Incredibly, against the background of impoverishment and pauperisation so far described, there is agreement amongst the statisticians and economists that the general level of life in Egypt, greatly improved in the last hundred years, is still tending to improve.

A country in the condition of Egypt badly needs a stroke of luck and it is actually possible that in the next few years Egypt may be lucky. With the return of the Sinai oil fields from Israeli occupation it is probable that Egyptian oil production may actually exceed the national consumption. Nor are the possibilities limited to the Sinai area; there is great and increasing interest among the oil prospectors in the Gulf of Suez; and in the Libyan desert the Egyptian experts have not given up the hope that on the Egyptian side of the frontier discoveries may be made on the same scale as those which have made the fortunes of Libya. It is possible, in fact, that the Egyptian economy may be saved by oil.

In the meantime the Egyptian government is busying itself with a more modest resource, the tourist industry. Tourists will not visit Egypt in order to look at oilfields. The attractions of the country as we have described them are astonishing, but of a decidedly specialised character. Additional boats are planned for the Nile trip and a new monster hotel at Luxor. An enormous tourist project was intended for a site adjacent to the plateau of the Giza pyramids: 10,000 beds, golf course, swimming pools, shopping centre and so on; but recently there appear to have been second thoughts. The major concentration inevitably is in Cairo itself; nine new grand hotels are planned to be in operation by 1981 and on the site of the old Omar Khayam palace in Gezira there is to be developed the largest hotel complex in the Middle East.

Innumerable books have been writen about Egypt, many of the highest quality, and it may be asked what justification there can be for yet another book. The answer, as this chapter has sought to show, is that modern Egypt is a country where in a steadily accelerating tempo events are constantly being overtaken by events. Until comparatively recent times, it was a general convention for the visitor that modern Egypt was an unsatisfactory development and had better be ignored. In times to come it is going to be increasingly difficult to ignore modern Egypt, and yet the tourist industry, if it is to be developed on the ambitious lines now planned, will still have to rely primarily on the Egyptian past.

To learn something of that past before embarking is an obviously sensible step. James Baikie's *Egyptian Antiquities in the Nile Valley* (Methuen), though dated as far back as 1932, is still an admirable description, compendious, interesting and readable, and it covers all the centuries of the Pharaohs and their Greek and Roman successors. In a very different category is Robert Curzon's *Visits to Monasteries in the Levant,* of which the fourth edition was published by Murray in 1851; this is a highly personal account of Curzon's visits to the Egyptian monasteries, both Orthodox and Coptic. Alexandria and Cairo are fortunate in having two of the world's best descriptive guide-books; E. M. Forster's *Alexandria; a History and a Guide,* published in 1938 and *Mediaeval Cairo,* published in 1962, a labour of love by Dorothea Russell, wife of Russell Pasha, the former English Commandant of the Cairo City Police. Bonaparte's expedition has recently been admirably re-written by J. Christopher Herold (Hamish Hamilton, 1962) in *Bonaparte in Egypt,* a study both comprehensive, penetrating and entertaining. Brian M. Fagan's *The Rape of the Nile* (Macdonald and Janes, 1977) is a splendid account of the early nineteenth-century spoliators. For later nineteenth-century travel I have drawn on a family book *Eau-de-Nil,* by E. C. Hope-Edwardes (1882). The classic exposition of the British occupation is to be found in Cromer's *Modern Egypt,* 1908, and Lloyd's *Egypt Since Cromer,* 1933, both published by

Macmillan, but these volumes cannot be recommended for light reading; interesting sidelights on the period can be found in Sir Philip Magnus's three biographies published by Murray: *Gladstone* (1954), *Kitchener* (1958) and *Edward VII* (1964). It is never easy to recommend books on the very recent past, but a topical note is struck by the President of Egypt's own book, *In Search of Identity.* A charming small vignette of the country is Robin Fedden's *Egypt* (Murray, 1977).

These books which the author has used and enjoyed are but a minute selection of the available literature. No object could be served by printing yet another bibliography of Egypt; they are only too easily to be found. The above selection does not include any professional guide books. Egypt, as has already been hinted, is not ready-made for this treatment; it is difficult here to do what is taken for granted in Western countries, wandering guide book in hand from monument to monument and city to city and absorbing the masterpieces from the printed word. Nevertheless there is a much-to-be-respected type of traveller for whom nothing replaces the guide book and for such a traveller the 1970s in Egypt have been an unfortunate decade. Baedeker, as always, is the most detailed and the most accurate and the last new edition of the book (originally printed in 1929) was in 1974 by David & Charles. The Guide Bleu, less detailed than Baedeker, is a good modern guide, but the Guide Bleu so far has not appeared in English.

For the visitor who has done some reading beforehand there is everything to be said for seeing the country, its monuments and people without the book. Not everything seen will be pleasant, there may even be moments of horror; these will tend to diminish as one removes oneself further from Cairo. It is impossible, if time allows, not to fall in love with the fellahin. Of all the disasters that could happen to modern Egypt none could be greater than the disruption of his age-old way of life. At all costs it is essential to preserve what economists would describe as the inefficient and primitive system of Egyptian agriculture; a modernisation of farming methods on the Western model would result in a massive uprooting of the population from the villages and the countryside, a tidal wave of indigent humanity descending upon the already hopelessly overstrained towns and cities of Egypt. In taking leave of this country and its people, let us express the hope that its people will reap the rewards of the energy and courage of its rulers and that its rulers will respect the ways of life and traditions of its people.

INDEX

Index of Subjects, *Persons* and PLACES
Numerals in *italics* indicate principal entries.

Abassids, 45
ABOUKIR BAY, 39, 41, 42, 50, 51
ABOUTIG, 115
ABU SIMBEL, *147-9*
ABUSIR, 41
ABYDOS, 17, 96, *116-9*
Aga Khan, tomb of, 142, 143
Ahmose, 20, 123, 125
Aida, 22, 68
Akhenaten, 22-3, 93, 96-7, 123, 137-8
ALAMEIN, 57; battle of, 65
Alexander the Great, 28-9, 30-1, 65, 124
ALEXANDRIA, *30-42*
   ancient sites, 40
   Arab conquest, 38
   Bonaparte at, 38-9
   Byzantine era, 37-8
   Christian era, 36-8
   environs, 41
   foundation, 30
   harbours, 31
   mouseion and library, 32
   museum, 41
   Pharos, 31
   plan, 31
   Pompey's pillar, 32
   Roman conquest, 34, 36
   Serapeum and Caesareum, 32
   Social life, 56
   Soma, 32
   under Mehemet Ali, 39-40
   under the Ptolemies, 33
Al-Hakim, 46
Ali, 45
AMARNA, 22, 90, 91, 93, *113-4*
Amenemmes I, 20, 128
Amenemmes III, 20
Ameni, tomb of, 111-2
Amenhotep, 138
Amenophis I, 20
Amenophis II, 21, 93, 127; tomb of, 133

Amenophis III, 21, 91, 93, 123, 127, 137
Amenophis IV, see Akhenaten
Americans, 58-9, 157
Amr, 45, 76, 80
Amun, 22, 23, 96-7, 123, 125
   priests of, 113
Anthony, Mark, 34
ANTINOOPOLIS, 113
Anubis, 96, 131
Apis, 96, 103
Arabs, 2-3, 156-7
Arianism, 37
Artaxerxes, 27
ASSIOUT, 114-5
ASSUAN, *142-4*
   dam, 55, 59, 69
   high dam, 146, 153
Assyrian Empire, 26
Aten, 22, 96, 114
Athanasius, 37
Augustus, 34, 35
Ayyubites, 47

BABYLON, 43, 76
Baikie, James, 147-8, 160
BALLIANA, 116
Baring, Sir Evelyn, see *Cromer*
Barkuk, 48, 85, 87
Beibars, 48
Belzoni, 53, 91, 133, 148
BENI HASAN, 20, 110-2
BENI SUEF, 19, 105
Bilharzia, 151-2
Bocchoris, 26
Bonaparte, Napoleon, 38-9, 50-1, 67, 75, 139
British 54-8, 68-9
British Museum, 52, 53, 66, 70, *90-1*
BUBASTIS, 24, 25, 62, 63, 67
BULAK, 72, 92

Caesar, Julius, 32, 34, 121
CAIRO, 71-89, 155

Abdin Palace, 75
   burning of, 57-8
   central quarters, 72, 73-4, 85-8
   Citadel, 70, 77, *83-5*
   Coptic museum, 80
   El-Azhar, 80-1
   European quarters, 74, 78
   Ezbekia, 73, 75
   Fatimid City, 86-7
   Gezira, 72, 74
   history, 76-7
   housing conditions, 72, 155
   Ibn Tulun, mosque of, 81-2
   Islamic museum, 88, 160
   Museum of Ancient Egypt, 74, 92-4
   Old Cairo, 72, 76, *78-80*
   population, 73
   Roda Island, 72
   Shepheard's hotel, 75
   social life, 56
   suburbs, 70
   Sultan Hasan, mosque of, 82-3
   Tahrir Square, 73
   Tombs of the Caliphs, 70, *85*
Cambyses, 27
Carter, Howard, 54
Chalcedon, Council of, 37
Champollion, 53
Cheops, 18, 19, 100-1
Chephren, 18, 92, 102
Clement, 37
Cleopatra, 32, *33-5,* 65, 121
Cleopatra's Needle, 99-100
Copts, 37, 78-80
Cotton, 52, 55, 60
CROCODILOPOLIS, 106
Cromer, Lord, 52, 54-5, 56, 160
Crusades, 46-7, 77
Curzon, Robert, 66, 145, 160
Cyprus, 26

Dahabichs, 55, 110

DAMIETTA, 61
Darius, 27, 67
DASHUR, 18, 20, 105
DEIR-EL-BAHARI, 131
DEIR-EL-BARSHA, 113
DEIR-EL-MEDINA, 135
Delta, the, 61-4; in time of
   Herodotus, 28
DENDERA, 119-21
Denon, 50-1
Desaix, General, 51, 145
Dhuthotep, tomb of, 113
Dragomaus, 55
Duff-Gordon, Lucy, 55

EDFU, 140-1
Edward VII, 55
Edwards, Amelia, 55
EGPLUM, 119
EL-AMARNA, see AMARNA
EL-AZHAR, Mosque of, 46, 72,
   80-1
ELEPHANTINE Island, 142-3
El-Ghuri, 48
Eratosthenes, 32
ESNA, 139-40
Ethiopian Dynasty, 26
Euclid, 32
Eugénie, Empress, 52, 68

Farouk, 57, 58
Fatimids, 46-7
FAIYUM, 20, 105-6
Fellahin, 107-8, 161
French, 38-9, 49-51, 124
Fuad, 56

Gnosticism, 37
Gorst, Eldon, 56
GOSCHEN, LAND of, 65, 67
Greeks, 26, 27, 59

Hadrian, 113, 137, 145
Hakim, 86
Haremhab, 129
Hasan, 48, 82, 83
Hathor, 96, 119-20, 131, 135, 149
Hatshepsut, 20-1, 111, 127, 128,
   129, *131*: temple of, 131-2
HAWARA, 20, 106
HELIOPOLIS, 71, *99*
HELOUAN, 60, 151
Heraclius, 38
HERACLEOPOLIS, 19, 105
Herihor, 25, 125
HERMOPOULIS, 113

Herodotus, 27-8, 61, 63, 67, 97,
   100, 106, 145
Hieroglyphics, 98-9
Hirkhouf, tomb of, 143
Hope-Edwardes, Ellen, 110, 160
Horemheb, 23, 24
Horus, 95-6, 119-20;
   statue of, 140
Hyskos, the, 20

Ibn Tulun, 45, 76, 81-2
Ibrahim Pasha, 51-2, *75*
Imhotep, 104
Isis, 95-6
Islam, 1-2, 44-5, 159
Ismail, 52, 54, 67-8, 75, 78
ISMAILIA, 69
Israel, 57, 58, 60, 154, 156-7
Italians, 64-5

Jerusalem, 46, 48, 157

Kadesh, battle of, 24
Kait Bey, 31, 85
Kalaoun, 48, 87
KANTARA, 70
KARNAK, 123, *125-9*
KATARA Depression, 65, 154
Khamsin, 13
KHARGALI, 27
Khons, 125
Kingston Lacy, 53, 100, 145
Kitchener, Lord, 12, 56
KITCHENER ISLAND, 143
KOM OMBO, 141-2

LABYRINTH, 20, 106
LAHOUN, 105, 106
Lesseps, Ferdinand de, 52, *67-8*
LIBYAN DESERT, 64-5
LISHT, 20
London, 32, 36, 100
Louis, Saint, 47, 61
Louvre, 53, 90, 134
LUXOR, 122; temple of, *123-5;*
   museums, 137-8

MALAWI, 113
Mamelukes, 47, 49, 51, 77
Manetho, 17
Mariette, 53, 92, 103
MARIOUT, LAKE, 39, 41, 61
Maspero, 54, 132, 134
MEDINET-EL-FAIYUM, 105
MEDINET HABU, 136-7
Mediterranean, 12-13, 152

Mehemet Ali, 39-40, *51-2,* 77, 83-4;
   mosque and tomb of, 83-4
MEIDUM, 18, 92, *105,* 106
MEMNON, COLOSSI OF, 22,
   130, *137*
Memnon, Young, 53, 91
MEMPHIS, 17, 26, 35, 96, 103,
   104-5
Menes, 17, 105
Menna, tomb of, 135
Mentuhotep II, 19, 131
Mentuhotep III, 19, 131
Mereruka, tomb of, 104
MERSA MATRUH, 65
Middle Kingdom, 19-20, 110-1
Mineptah, 25
Monophysism, 37
Mont, Temple of, 128
MONTAZAH, 42
Moses, 70
Moslems, see Islam
Mussolini, 57, 65
Mut, temple of, 129
Mykerinos, pyramid of, 102

Nakht, tomb of, 135
Nasir, 48, 87
Nasser, Gamal Abdel, 57-60, 147
   155
NASSER, LAKE, 150-1
NAUCRATIS, 26, 62
Necho, 67
Nectanebis II, 91, 141, 145-6
Nefertiti, 114
Neguib, 58
New York, 32, 36, 99
Nile, 107-9
   birds of, 109
   fish of, 109
   inundations, 16-7, 150-1
   upper waters, 153
Nile, Battle of the, 39, 50
Nilometers, 80, 141, 143
Nur-ed-din, 47

Obelisks, 99-100, 124, 127, 144
Octavian, see Augustus
Origen, 37
Osiris, 95-6, 97, 116
Overland route, 30

PANOPOLIS, 115
Papyri, 91, 98
Pekhet, 111
PELUSIUM, 70
Pepi II, 19

Persian Empire, 26, 28, 38
Petosiris, 113
Petrie, Sir Flinders, 54
PHAROS, 31
PHILAE, 144-6
Piankhi, 26
PITHON, 64
Pocock, Richard, 49
Population, 153, 158
PORT SAID, 30, 68, 69
Psammeticus I, 26
Psammeticus III, 26
Ptah, 17, 96, 128
Ptahhotep, tomb of, 104
Ptolemy I, 31
Ptolemy II, 146
Ptolemy IV, 135
Ptolemaic dynasty, 33, 35
PTOLEMAIS, 116
Punt, land of, 21, 93, 131
Pyramids, 18
   battle of, 50
   of Abusir, 103
   of Dashar, 105
   of Giza, 100-3
   of Meidum, 105
   of Sakkara, 103

Quarries of Assuan, 144
Qus, 17

RAAMSES, 64
Rameses I, 23, 116, 126
Rameses II, 23-25, 116, 117-9,
   124, 127, 148-9; funeral
   temple, 135
Rameses III, 25, 125, 126, 136-7;

   tomb of, 134
Rameses VI, tomb of, 134
RAMLAH, 42
Ramose, tomb of, 135

Septimius Severus, 137, 139
Serapeum, 103
Sesostris I, 20, 93
Sesostris II, 20, 112
Sesostris III, 20, 91
Seth, 95-6
Seti I, 23, 24, 53, 116, 117, 118,
   127, 130; tomb of, 133-4
Sheshonk, 25, 126, 127
SIDI BARRANI, 64, 65
SIDFA, 115
SIHEL Island, 144
SINAI, 59, 69-70
Sirenpont I and II, tombs of,
   143
SIWA, Oasis of, 65
Snefru, 17, 105
Soane museum, 133
SOHAG, 115
SOLLUM, 65
Sphinx, 102
Strabo, 106, 123
Sudan, 151-3
SUEZ, 30, 69
Suez campaign, 59, 69
Suez Canal, 30, 59, 60, 67-9
Sugar, 112
Syria, 60

Tahaska, 26
TANIS, 25, 62, 63
TAPHANES, 64

TAPOSIRIS MAGNA, 41
Temples, Egyptian, 117
Tewfik, 52
THEBES, 19, 122-3, 129-37
THINIS, 116
Thoth, 96, 113
TONNAL-EL-GEBEL, 113
TOSA, 115
Tourist Industry, 159-60
Trajan, 67
Turks, 47, 48-51, 55, 77
Tutankhamen, 23, 54, *93-4,* 128;
   tomb of, 133
Tutankhaten, see Tutankhamen
Tuthmosis I, 20, 127, 131, 132
Tuthmosis II, 20, 128, 131
Tuthmosis III, 21, 93, 111, 128,
   131; tomb of, 131-2
Tuthmosis IV, 21

Umaiyads, 45, 76
Unas, pyramid of, 104
UNESCO, 147, 148

VALLEY OF THE KINGS, 21,
   97, *132-4*
VALLEY OF THE QUEENS,
   136

WADI NATROUN,
   Monasteries of, 65-6
WESTERN DESERT,A 64-5
Wilkinson, Sir Gardner, 53

Zagloul, Suad, 56
Zer, 116
Zoser, 17, 103, 104, 116